UNDERSTANDING POVERTY

By the Same Author

1. Environment and Sustainable Development (2000)
2. Development Economics (1999)
3. Reforming World Economies: Lessons for India (1997)
4. India's Economic Reforms and Beyond (1995)

UNDERSTANDING POVERTY

R.K. SINHA

ANAMIKA PUBLISHERS & DISTRIBUTORS (P) LTD.
4697/3, 21A, Ansari Road, Daryaganj
New Delhi 110002
Phones: 3201531, 3281655

First Published 2003

ISBN 81-7975-018-3

PRINTED IN INDIA

Published by Anamika Publishers & Distributors (P) Ltd., 4697/3, 21A, Ansari Road, Daryaganj, New Delhi 110002. Typeset by Veronica Grafic Arts, MU-61D, Vishakha Enclave, Delhi 110034 and Printed at Nagri Printers, Delhi.

Preface

A decade of economic reforms and globalisation like planned developments finds itself unable to meet the challenges of poverty. We stand at the beginning of a new millennium, which provides us an opportunity to assess where we had been and where we are now as well as to provide a vision for the future for meeting the challenge of poverty.

Poverty haunts the lives of nearly one-third people of India and of billion of people around world. Despite the general trends of liberalising global economic expansion, markets, and increased trade, poverty still restrict the choices, freedom and longevity of millions.

Poor people live without fundamental freedoms of action and choice that the better off take for granted. They often lack adequate food and shelter, education and health, deprivation that keep them from leading the kind of life that everyone values. They also face extreme vulnerability to ill-health, economic dislocations and natural disasters. They are also exposed to ill treatment by institutions of the State and society and they are powerless to influence key decisions affecting their lives. These are many facets of poverty, which have been the subject-matter of the treatise on understanding poverty. This will give an insight in understanding the problem of poverty and the solution thereof. It will be very useful for our political leadership, planners and policy-makers.

I have been much benefited from the writing and discussion with Dr. Man Mohan Singh, Dr. P.R. Brahmananda and Dr. V.R. Panchmukhi which have sharpen my understanding on poverty. I owe a heavy debt to them. I am also indebted to Sri Madan Lal of World Bank for providing the materials and to Dr. M.K. Singh, Sri Subodh Dhawan, Md. Ishrar Khan of the department for their help. I am thankful to Sri Manoj Kumar Pandey for typing the manuscript.

Last but not to least I owe heavy debt to my wife Dr. Madhuri Sinha, son Mr. Ardhendhu Shekhar and daughter Miss Akanksha Shekhar who kept me fighting fit.

R.K. Sinha

Contents

1

Introduction

We stand at the beginning of a new millennium at the end of a decade when globalisation has accelerated dramatically. This a time to assess where we have been as well as to provide a vision for the future for eradication of poverty. This is a time of great opportunity but also of great challenges.

A decade ago, globalisation was considered for India as an opportunity and poverty as our challenges. Yet a decade of globalisation has failed to have its impact on the poor.

Globalisation is about an increasingly interconnected and interdependent world, it is about international trade, investment and finance that have been growing faster than incomes of individual nations. It is about new opportunities for people in all countries to develop their potential and to support their families through employment opportunities created for them by greater economic integration. Contrary to this expectation, people in developing countries often fear losing of employment opportunities because of high skilled manpower requirements and fear of losing employment opportunities, which they have.

No doubt, in an unequal world globalisation is about risks as well as full of opportunities. The risks are larger for the developing countries and these have to be tackled at national levels by managing adjustment process and by strengthening social, structural and financial systems. At the global level, there is need to establish a stronger international financial architecture, and work to fight poverty through human development.

In an unequal world, we live in a country which itself has been divided between urban rich and rural poor. The richest

20 per cent receives more than 80 per cent of the incomes. The gap between the average incomes of 20 per cent rich and 20 per cent poor is widening. The average annual increase in employment opportunities in India has declined from 1.44 per cent in 1991 to 0.4 per cent by the turn of the century.

With all the forces working for integrating India with the world must think first to integrate rural Bharat with urban India. It is time to change our thinking. It is time to realise that we should live together. The political leadership must realise this reality and must not divide the country's social fabric just for lust of power. The conflicts that have so plagued socio-economic polity are not simply accidents of history. It has been caused by great divide between rich and poor.

Neither market nor State alone is capable of fighting poverty. The markets as well as the State have failed to find a sustainable solution of poverty. Market represents profit and profit is possible only in an unequal society. Whereas State represents equality and do the work of creating an enabling environment for people to live a long, healthy and creative life.

No doubt, poverty is about more than inadequate income or even low human development, it is also about lack of voice, lack of representation. It is about vulnerability to abuse and to corruption. Despite the general trends of global economic expansion, liberalising markets, and increased trade, poverty still restricts the choices, freedom and longevity of billions of people in the world and nearly one-third in India.

Without development of social infrastructure only provision of economic infrastructure is not a sufficient condition for sustainable growth and development. Economic infrastructure may increase growth but at the same time it would widen inequalities and regional imbalances. Even in highly developed countries public expenditure on the social sector constitutes a substantial part of resource allocation. For example, in 1996-97, public allocation for health and education in France was 13.7 per cent of GDP, 12 per cent in U.S.A., 11.1 per cent in the U.K., 6.6 per cent in Malaysia and 4.1 per cent in Sri Lanka. While over the years public expenditure on the social sector and poverty alleviation has increased in absolute terms, but, the rate of increase during the reforms period has been declining.

II

Economic growth without social justice has no relevance for socio-economic polity of India. An unequal and unbalanced socio-economic policy cannot be content merely with the target of economic growth and increase in production. What is important is to ensure equitable distribution and alleviation of poverty. This is possible only by the State in a planned way. This needs a philosophy and development perspective, this was indeed behind the thinking of both Gandhi and Nehru and the Indian Constitution. Today, no one seems to remember Gandhi's criteria for choice, viz., that while taking economic decisions, the planners or the administrator, as the case may be, must think in terms of giving priority to helping the poor out of their poverty. The absence of philosophy of development in recent years is highly regrettable. Quantitative targets without regard for the distributional implications are creating an environment within the country that has become allergic to growth as it does not involve either mass participation or fulfilment of mass needs.

At the dawn of Independence, the nation had many priorities and problems to tackle. Important among them were national integration, the role to be assigned to the people in the government and economic and social development. Although these problems are inter-linked in terms of solution, while they need to be tackled individually, they also needed to be dealt with in a coordinated and integrated manner. Unfortunately, the first two did not receive the attention they deserved which has created many new problems today. National integration has taken for granted, while the active role that people should play in government was not given much attention. Attention was concentrated only on economic development.

People in an independent country were expecting freedom to bring about a nationally-oriented utilisation of natural and human resources, a substantial increase in national product, a significant rise in their well-being and eradication of poverty and unemployment. To fulfil this aspiration, economic growth became the major goal. While selecting the strategy for growth, the leadership was much influenced by the then existing world economic environment. Moreover, the economic growth became the yardstick for measuring national achievements and in the process the people's aspirations were either taken for granted or considered to be a by-product.

No doubt, during the post-reform era there have been a considerable increase in national product, there has also been a perceptible increase in per capita income. At the same time, the decline in the poverty of masses has not been significant, nor has there been any noticeable movement towards reducing inequalities in income and wealth in the country. The pre-reform achievements have been, summarised in the following words by Prof. V.K.R.V. Rao:

> It is true that production increased, and with it a pale imitation of Western affluence, sometimes conspicuously vulgar, appear in the country. Large houses, modern hotels, fleets of cars and tarred roads for travel and shops for the sale of luxury goods came up, but these were outside the preview of the poor masses, who became either passive and awe-struck with admiration, were imbued with inner resentment that spent itself in futile lobgesang and non-participant or decadening role in national economic development.[1]

III

There was no mala fide intention on the part of the ruling class in the country. Economic growth, they considered as a diffusionary process that would automatically spill over areas and classes, and would give the masses of the population as well as all the areas in the country a significant share of its dividends. In reality, this did not happen. Oasis of affluence and economic well-being surrounded by Saharas of poverty and economic backwardness appeared in India. The nation was divided between urban rich and the rural poor. No doubt, the theorists of growth have also changed their perception and given up their belief in its automatic diffusionary effects over all the regions and people of the country. They shifted towards providing an in-built elements in the growth process that would lead to a more equitable distribution of income and assets for eradicating poverty and maintaining employment.

However, the path of development which was followed in

the country was based on a mistaken application of Western model of development involving capital intensity use of modern technology and urbanisation without taking into account our abundant labour supply, the extensive prevalence of illiteracy and the lack of skills among our labour force, the predominantly rural character of our population and the prevalence of commercial rather than an industrial bias in our entrepreneurship. The capitalist developed world took many decades to develop their industry and urban civilisation. Their transition from original rural status made possible by the absence of a parliamentary democracy, lack of class consciousness among their working class and/or organisation on their part, and the absence of an informed and progressive public opinion. Their problem of initial capital accumulation had also been solved by their conquest of colonisation of the countries. Combining this with their advance in science and technology and with the dynamism and austerity of their early capitalist class they were able to achieve a rate of economic growth and a level of national income which took them beyond the demographic transition state, and enabled them to go ahead with their capital intensive production and allied use of labour-saving technology.

Not taking into consideration the socio-economic-politico environments of India and ignoring the hard reality of our own history, we derive the lesions from history of development in the Western world. Soon after Independence we opted for a model of growth that was based on capital intensive industry, neglect of agriculture and the masses who worked in the agriculture and rural areas, and failed to develop the human resource potential in their abundant labour supply. Neglecting human resource development we embarked on a programme of capital intensive economic development that necessitated large scale dependence on foreign aid in both capital and technology and brought demonstration effect of Western affluence and its corrupting effects on our domestic elites. Naturally, this economic approach to development, based on model unsuited to our social, economic and resource conditions, led to the creation of highly unequal society, with pockets of affluence mainly confined to urban areas, rural stagnation, growing unemployment and continuing poverty among the masses. The result was disillusionment and a search for alternative ways of development.

IV

Development is creating an environment for people to live a long healthy and creative lives. The model of development requires that priority attention be paid to such factors as illiteracy, lack of industrial or technical skills, vast inequality in the possession of not only land but also of other productive assets, and dominance of agriculture and the rural sector in the economy with distressingly low output for worker. Non-consideration of these factors in the model that was followed led to more one of confusion than of ideological confrontation and lack of a clear understanding among people of the ideological implications of development on their own welfare and their own role as an active participants, in the development process.

The development model that was followed was a mixture of two ideologies on the one hand, from the Western capitalist system, we borrowed their political system of parliamentary democracy, adult franchise, periodic elections and fundamental rights. We also shared with the Western economic system their private property and a large role for private enterprise and the profit motive, not only in agriculture but also in industry, trade, service and other sectors of economic activity. On the other hand, from the socialist model, we borrowed central planning, dominant role of public sector in industry, transport, energy and credit and public regulation of private economic activity administered prices, a battery of controls and bulging bureaucracy. However, neither we had the advantage of a social and economic revolution preceding development nor did we support development process with the necessary institutional change in social relations and property rights or an understanding and positive participation by the people. And no attention was given to human resource development. As a matter of fact we succeeded in setting up the formal framework of a socialist pattern within the context of a mixed economy and a parliamentary democracy, but utterly failed to bring about a social transformation of our society and the development of our human resources. There has been growth but it has not been accompanied by social justice.

I do not support the views that our decision to go in for a mixed economy to secure economic growth with social justice was wrong but where we did go wrong was the choice of strategy of planning giving dominance to public sector in all economic activities. We forget the historical truth that the State agençies and the public sector provide external economies to a fast growing private sector and offer no effective opposition to the increasing concentration of economic power in private hands. Contrary to this, we accorded public sector the status of commanding heights to determine the main direction of economic development. Our experiment with mixed economy could have been based on historical truth. However, in place of having a mixed economy, we mixed up everything with giving commanding height of the economy to the public sector. Consequently, we failed to bring about the desired social transformation. The failure was further facilitated by the power structure of a mixed economy functioning under parliamentary democracy.

What was wrong, therefore, was not so much the framework of the strategy as the neglect of its political economy. The missing link in the development strategy has been the absence of mobilisation of the political, social, ethical and cultural forces needed for socialist transformation.

Our experiences of pre- and post-reform period amply demonstrate that under a purely economic or purely political pattern of parliamentary democracy, social justice, economic growth process is bound to be thwarted by vested interests and the power structure on the non-economic plan. In order to secure social justice what is needed most along with economic growth is a comprehensive and integrated approach to development.[2]

In short, the failure was caused partly by the authorities not taking into account the effect of unequal distribution of productive assets and the social political and economic conditions of the rural masses which thwarted the achievement of social justice and partly the freedom conferred on private enterprise did not help the poor but led to the strengthening of vested interests in the rural economy and the creation of a powerful Kulak class that inevitably had the impact on the rural power structure to the detriment of the rural poor and social justice which they were entitled.

Both in the pre- and post-reform periods growth strategy, the political and economic freedom embodied in political democracy has been a fertile ground for the dominance of the socio-political system by vested interests and the elite and the privileged class who used the framework of the political system to strengthen their control over the power structure and their share in the dividends from economic growth at the expense of the masses who have been given a titular right to vote them out of political power. The failure to take into account the hard reality led even well-intentioned economic planning and freedom enshrined in political democracy to fill and make us to stand in the queue for foreign aid and borrowing with all implications for national sovereignty and to opt for deficit financing and inflation while at the same time failing to solve the problems of mass poverty and unemployment.

V

The performance of Indian economy during the last fifty years clearly indicate that neither planning nor the free economy has been able to make any significant impact on the poor. If we assess correctly gains of the processes of development which has been under way, one may conclude that the basic structural problems of the society has always been bypassed. For making possible economic and social development along with equity and social justice, what is needed most is the involvement of people in the development process. The people at large have to be made aware and accept the implications of development with equity. At the same time, we have to dissociate the concept of freedom from that of economic freedom associated with private enterprise, market forces and the profit maximising motive and place it on a firm footing of social equity, reduction of economic disparities within the limits of tolerance and functional efficiency, equity of opportunity, concern for the maintenance of cultural diversities and non-disruptive social deviance, encouragement of creativity and innovative directed to the development goals.

While determining economic targets for development, we should primarily take into account the limit set out by our human and natural resources and the need for fostering self-reliance and abandoning dependence. The goal of economic development must be to give all the people in the country a reasonable national minimum living standard and a happy and culturally satisfying life, rather than the multitude of material possessions associated with Western capitalist affluence and its social and psychological tensions.

Whatever path one may follow, one should not forget that development is for the promotion of domestic human welfare and not for the sacrifice of the citizen at the alter of the competitive rising of economic growth rates. Development is an environment for people to live a long, healthy and creative lives. Such an environment is possible if there exists nutrition, health, literacy, skills, education, culture, social awareness, humaneness, compassion, fraternity, secularism, respect for human dignity, self-reliance and the work ethic.

Market or globalisation cannot create such an environment for a society divided between few rich and large poor. There is no escape from planning, if development is to succeed in achieving its goals but planning should leave adequate scope for effective decentralisation that could release the dormant emerges of the people and secure their active participation in local and regional development.

Problem of poverty cannot be solved with globalisation of Indian economy. Indian should rethink on economic reforms and back to the middle path. There are deep-seated class biases in the pressures that are determining the national priorities and that inequalities in education, health and opportunities are in fact, a reflection of inequalities of economic and social power of different groups in India.

This needs a change for tackling the problem of poverty.

NOTES AND REFERENCES

1. Rao, V.K.R.V., "Economic Growth and Social Justice" in R. Bhardwaj (*et al.*) *Planning for Economic and Social Development* (1992), Sage, New Delhi, p. 33.
2. Such an approach would take into account not only economic

factors relevant to growth or political factors pertinent to a parliamentary democracy, but also the socio-cultural factors relevant to both justice and growth. The direct and indirect influence exerted by vested interest, the compassion and bias of power structure and all other variables in the way of social transformation.

2

Poverty, Deprivation and Development

> Poverty is hunger, loneliness, nowhere to go when the day is over, deprivation, discrimination, abuse and illiteracy.

It is the deprivation of lives that people can lead that poverty manifests itself. Poverty can involve not only the lack of well-being but the denial of opportunities for living a tolerable life.[1] No doubt living standards has risen dramatically over last 25 years, the numbers of people living in poverty continues to grow. As a result, the proportion of the poor is holding steadily at less than a third of the developing world's population. More than 1.3 billion people in the developing world still struggle to survive on less than a dollar a day and the number continues to increase.

The poor usually lack assets as well as income. In agrarian economies in which wealth and status come from the land, disadvantaged households are typically land-poor or landless. Since they lack income and access to credit, they are usually unable to improve their position in the societal structure. They also lack in human capital. Everywhere they have a lower level of educational access and lower achievement than the population at large. Everywhere the poor have been deprived of access to land and avenues for human capital formation. Agriculture is still the main source of income for them. Even within the agriculture, there are two groups of poor—the self-employed and the wage labourers. Two important determinants of poverty are access to income earning opportunities and the capacity to respond. Where households have secure opportunities to use their labour for good purposes and are skilled, educated, and healthy, minimal standards of living are ensured and poverty is eliminated. Where such opportunities are lacking and access to social services are limited, living standards are usually low.

The living standards of many in developing countries are also highly vulnerable to a variety of misfortunes, ranging from illness to drought. Inability to cope with shocks often render relatively well of households poor and lead to starvation and death for those already impoverished.

The poor have been deprived of their entitlements in both the capitalist and socialist system as both the systems have failed to arrive at a balance between growth and development. The growth depends greatly on the marginal property to save. Higher the growth rate of marginal propensity to save higher will be the rate of investment, which will result in higher growth of the economy. Country development depends on the marginal propriety to consume. Higher the marginal propriety to consume of the people, it will lead to their better health, education and increase in their standard of living. Better educated and healthy manpower will spur the growth. Without growth development is not possible so also without development growth is not possible. Market and State must move hand in hand. Efficient market and capable State are the most efficient pillars of economic development. Market stimulates growth and State stimulates development. Unless a society is developed growth is not possible and in the absence of growth development of the society is also not possible.

Development is not growth alone. It is growth plus change in values and institutes. Unless a part of the growth is used for changing the values and institutions, growth will result is social deprivation for a large number of people.

The people who have been deprived of their entitlement are poor. Entitlement relations accepted in a market economy typically include, among others:

1. ***Trade-based Entitlement:*** One is entitled to own what one obtains by trading something what one owns with a willing party/parties.
2. ***Production-based Entitlement:*** One is entitled to own

what one gets by arranging production using one's owned resources, or resources hired from willing parties meeting the agreed conditions of trade.

3. ***Own-labour Entitlement:*** One is entitled to one's own labour power, and thus to the trade-based and production-based entitlements related to one's labour power.
4. ***Inheritance and Transfer Entitlement:*** One is entitled to own what is willingly given to one by another who legitimately owns it, possible to take effect after the latter's death.

Socialist economy, on the other hand, does not permit private ownership of means of production thereby rendering 'production-based entitlements' inoperative accept when it involves just one's labour and some elementary tools and raw materials. Although both the capitalist and the socialist economies do not permit the ownership of one person by another, as slave economy do. A socialist economy restricts the employment of one person by another for production purposes. However, a capitalist economy does it by imposing restrictions on binding contracts involving labour-power obligations over long period of time.

The factors influencing the determination of a person's exchange entitlement, given his ownership bundle are:

(i) Whether he can find an employment, and if so for how long and at what wage rate;
(ii) What he can earn by selling his non-labour assets, and how much it costs him to buy whatever he may wish to buy;
(iii) What he can produce with his own labour power and resources he can buy and manage;
(iv) The cost of purchased resources and the value of the products he can sell;
(v) The social security benefits he is certified to and the taxes, etc., he pays.

The exchange entitlements of a person in a market economy very much depends on his position in the economic class structure as well as the modes of production in the economy, what he owns will also very with his class, and even if exactly the same E-mapping were to hold for all, the actual exchange entitlements worked differ with his ownership position. However, even with the same ownership position, the exchange entitlement, will be different depending on what economic prospects are open to him, and that will depend on the modes of production relations.

In fact, for an understanding of poverty, it is necessary to look at both ownership patterns and exchange entitlements and at the forces that lie behind them. However, the exchange entitlements depend not merely on market exchanges but also on the exchanges, if any, that the State provides as a part of its social security programme. Given a social security system, the unemployed portion may get relief, and old person a pension, and the poor some specified "benefits". They are parts of an exchange entitlements and are conditional in the absence of other exchanges that a person might undertake. A person's ability to possess any commodity for material benefits depends much on the entitlements relations that govern possession and use in that society. It depends on what he owns, what exchange possibilities are offered to him, what is given to him free and what is taken away from him. It is the totality of entitlement relations that govern whether a person will have the ability to acquire enough material to avoid poverty.

Income may be means to acquire material benefits but much will depend on its purchasing power. Though incomes do give one entitlement for material possession in a market economy, it may not provide command in a fully planned economy in which a different system of entitlement might hold good. No doubt, income does provide command, it offers only a part of picture of the entitlement pattern, and starting the story with the shortage of income is to leave the tale half-told.

Understanding entitlement approach needs just understanding of discrimination. A small peasant and a landless labourer may both be poor but their fortunes are not tied together. In understanding the prowess of their poverty: one has to view them not as a member of the huge army of the poor but as a member of particular classes belonging to particular occupational groups, having different ownership endowments and being govern by different entitlement relations. Dividing the population into the rich and the poor may serve specific purpose in a specific context; it is far too indiscriminating to be helpful in analysing poverty.

A Move Towards Entitlements

In a march toward eradicating poverty, everywhere the starting point must be to empower women and men and to ensure their participation in decisions that affect their lives and emulate them to build their strength and assets. Poor people and poor communities rely primarily on their own energy, creativity and assets. Such assets are not just economic. They are also social, political and environmental and personal. A people-centred strategy for eradicating poverty should start by building the assets of the poor and restoration of their entitlements and empowering them to win their fight against poverty.

The strategy for the restoration of entitlements and empowering the poor and the disadvantaged should consists—

1. Political commitment to securing and protecting the political, economic, social and civil rights of poor and disadvantaged people.
2. Policy reforms and actions to enable them to gain access to assets the absence of which make them more vulnerable. Security of tenure for housing and land is an important as access to credit and other financial services.
3. Education and health care for all, along with reproductive health services, family planning and safe water and sanitation needs to be achieved soon.
4. Social security nets to prevent people from falling into destitution and to rescue them from disaster.

Gender equality is essential for empowering women and for eradicating poverty. The burnt of poverty has been felt most by the women as they are being deprived of their legitimate entitlement. They are being on the frontline of household and community efforts to escape poverty and cope with its impact. But too often they do not have a voice in decision-making. Gender equality needs to be part of our strategy for eradicating poverty both as an end and as a means to eradicating other forms of human poverty.

A creative commitment to gender equality will strengthen every area of action to reduce poverty as women will be able to bring new energy, new insight, and a new basis for organisation, which alone will transform growth into development.

Only development of human capital can transform potential into reality. Economic growth contributes most to poverty reduction when it expands to employment, productivity and wages of poor and when public resources are channel for promoting human development. If poverty is to be reduced, policy-makers must avoid "ruthless" growth that leads to increasing income inequality. Contrary to some perceptions, inequality usually hinders growth.

Since most of the poor live in rural areas and mostly depend for their survival on agriculture, poverty eradication should begin from agriculture, which alone can raise the income of rural poor. Basic education and health are among the most powerful forces for raising productivity in the rural sector. Raising productivity will raise their income. Accelerated action to reduce human deprivation in education and health is a near universal need and should not wait for growth to resume.

Market and State: The Trade Off

Entitlement and deprivation much depends on the trade off between the market and the State. Economy grows and society develops. Unless a part of the growth spreads over the society, growth cannot be transformed into development. Growth is highly individualistic. It grows like a tree. A growing tree never thinks about the smaller one beneath it. To protect the smaller one, we need a gardener who take care of them. In the absence of a gardener, the stronger one survives and weaker one are deprived of their entitlements and such a system is known as "jungle raj". Deprivation happens when the rule of law do not operate.

Perspectives on Poverty

Perspectives on poverty are multi-dimensional. A person is

poor if his income is below the defined poverty line. Often the cut-off poverty line is defined in terms of having enough income for a specified amount of food.

Poverty is deprivation of material requirements for minimally acceptable fulfilment of human needs, including food. This concept of "derivative" goes well beyond the lack of income. It includes the need for basic health and education and essential services that have to be provided by the society to prevent people from falling into poverty. It also recognises the need for employment and participation.

Poverty represents the absence of such basic capabilities to function. The functioning can vary from such physical ones as being well nourished, being adequately clothed, and sheltered and avoiding preventable mobility, to more complex social achievements.

These may be called income perspective, basic needs perspectives and capability perspective. However, the capability approach reconcile the notions of absolute and relative poverty, since relative deprivation in income and commodities can lead to an absolute deprivation in minimum capabilities.

The Politics of Deprivation and Poverty

Politics, not just economics determines the deprivation and poverty. And what is lacking is not the economic resources on the economic solutions but a strong political will and action plan. Much is known about what is needed to eliminate deprivation and eradicate poverty jobled growth, access to credit redistribution of land, investment in social services, promotion of the informal sector, sound macroeconomic policies and the rule of law.

In this direction too little attention has been paid. How can an environment be which can ensure restoration of entitlements, elimination of deprivation and eradication of poverty. This to happen needs a political strategy having elements of political empowerment of deprived, partnership for change and an enabling and responsible State. The deprived must organise for collective action to influence the circumstances and decisions affecting their lives. To advance their interests, their voice must be heard in the corridors of power.

All agents in society need to come together in a partnership to address human deprivation in all its dimensions. Society must be open enough to tolerate a complex vying interests and coalition and to ensure stability and progress towards human development.

The most essential environment of this political strategy needs is a capable State and the need to foster peaceful expression of people's priorities and to ensure a democratic space for brokering the interests of society's many groups. The State needs to promote participation and encourage private public partnership, it also needs to be transparent and to resist pressure from the economically powerful.

A Formidable Task

Building peaceful political momentum for restoration of entitlement and eliminating deprivation is a formidable task. As stated in the outset that it is in the deprivation of the lives of people that poverty manifests itself. And poverty often serves the vested interests of the economically powerful, who frequently benefit from exploiting them. No doubt, poor people are often seen as an economic burden on society. Yet it often serves the vested interests of the economically powerful who depend on them to ensure that their society run smoothly. A mobile pool of low-paid and unorganised workers is useful doing the "dirty dangerous and difficult work" that others refuse to do. With no legal protection and opportunity for collective action they are exploited and paid low-wages being denied of their entitlement.

The poor are also politically convenient. They serve as scapegoats for the ills of society. They also serve as a useful pool of voters for politicians who promise to serve their interests.

Unless social, economic and political deprivation is eliminated and entitlement is restored by redistribution the resources and opportunities, eradication of poverty will remain a distant dream. This to happen will be resisted at all levels by the vested interests. Any strategy to eradicate poverty must therefore take into account the fact that many people have a vested interest in the perpetuation of poverty.

The realities of economic, social and political disparities and injustices are so overwhelming that few believe that things can change. And some think that only violence and confrontation can produce real change in favour of poor. Poverty is brutal. It can provide violent reactions.

Economy grows society develops, society develops by making progress in human development. History is replete with examples that human poverty has often resulted in uprising and rebellions against States that have advanced the interests of the economically powerful while tolerating rigid class division, unbearable economic conditions and human suffering and poverty. English peasants revolted against an impoverishing poll tax in 1381. German peasants rose up against their feudal overlords in opposition to serfdom in 1524. India too has a long tradition of peasants movements. As far back as in the 17th and 18th centuries, peasants rose up against the British Empire. Naxalite movement, in certain parts of India during post-Independence, is the manifestation of extreme injustices in the society and resultant of the poverty.

Full scale revolution have their roots in people's reaction to poverty and economic deprivation. Spontaneous uprisings instigated the French Revolution in 1789. The revolutionary movements across Europe in 1858 and the Bolshevik Revolution in 1917. The war of independence in Africa and Asia in the 19th and 20th centuries were not only the expression of nationalisation—they were also a struggle against social and economic deprivation and injustices. The civil right movement in the United States in the 1960s too was a struggle for social and economic emancipation.

However, not all process in social and economics emancipation was achieved through confrontation. Sometimes it was gradual and peaceful. The need of hour is peaceful and fundamental reform through collective action and people's participation. The challenge facing today's leaders, activists and people at large is to learn from the history and work towards non-violent change understanding the risks of confrontation and the backlashes it can produce. In fact, avoiding violence and chaos is in all people's interest and imperative of avoiding disorder must be the motivation to share power more equitably.

Emancipation from social, economic and political deprivation depends first and foremost on people's ability to articulate their demands and mobilise for collective actions. Isolated and deprived poor people have no power and no influence over political decisions that affect their lives. But organised, they have the power to ensure that their interests are advanced. It is the pressure from people to defend their rights and to remove obstacles and enhance their life opportunities that will emancipate them from deprivation, injustices and will eradicate human poverty.

Those who have been deprived must mobilise themselves and build solidarity to improve their life opportunities. Individual empowerment is the starting point of community action. Empowerment is about change in favour of those who previously exercised little control over their lives. This has two sides the first is the control over resources—financial, physical and human. The second is control over ideology—beliefs, values and attitudes. Empowerment starts with changes in consciousness and in self-perception. It taps powerful reservoirs of hope and enthusiasm among people used to viewing themselves negatively.

A vibrant civil society working towards emancipation of deprived and poor also depends on the mobilisation of people in more formal organisation. Poor people, however, well organised alone cannot force the policy shift for their social, economic and political emancipation without the support from other groups. Alliances, partnership and compromises are the only vehicle for peaceful, sustained reform. A clear shared vision of the future can alone provide unshakable focus for action. Reformers need to work-out the best strategy for negotiating their way through the power structure.

No doubt individuals and groups can do a great deal on their own to emancipate from deprivation. However, much will depend on the environment created by government action. The State has a central role not just through its influence on many elements of society and the call for people's mobilisation must not be a justification for the State to abdicate its responsibilities.

The strategy for empowering the deprived required not a retreating weak State but an active strong one, and that strength should be used to enable the poor rather than disable them.

Incapable States do the just opposite. They use much of their power for action that run counter to the interest of deprived and poor. In such a State politicians use government resources to strengthen their hold on power. Public officials demand bribe before they allow access to government benefits and well connected people use political influence to get preferential access to public resources. These lead to not just inefficient and inequitable allocation of resources, but also less freedom and more human deprivation.

In worst case politician have used their offices ruthlessly to amass personal wealth and power and benefit those on whose support this depend with no reward for efficiency or the public interest.

Ending human deprivation requires an activist State to create the political conditions for fundamental reform. Above all this requires a democratic space in which people can articulate demands, act collectively and fight for a more equitable distribution of power. Only then will adequate resources be invested in human development, priorities and access to productive assets become more equitable. Only when market become efficient and State capable, economy grows and society develops. Sustainability in growth and development results in ending economic and political deprivation.

Human poverty is the deprivation of human rights. Economic growth leads to social development only when a part of growth is used for human development. For emancipating people from deprivation and poverty we must empower individuals, households and communities to gain greater control over their life and resources and strengthen gender equality to empower women to release their vast underused energy and creativity.

Clear vision, strong political will and pro-poor strategy will bring change in the social, political and economic structure which alone can bring a sustainable growth and development.

Poverty in India

Removal of poverty and attainment of full employment has been the twin prime objectives of the Indian Five-Year Plans.

Indian Five-Year Plans have accorded great importance to poverty reduction to measure its success in achieving this goal. The government commissioned a series of household survey on poverty since 1957. These surveys provide an unparalleled record of India's efforts to reduce poverty.[2]

No doubt, India has reduced poverty in terms of percentage of population living below poverty line, but progress has been uneven over time and across States and the number of poor has continued to rise albeit at a slower rate. In 1950-51, the average head count index of poverty was 53 per cent, about the same as in 1970-74. Since then poverty incidence declined fairly steadily from its earlier range of 54 per cent in 1973-74 to 38 per cent in 1986-87. However, because of poor weather conditions and the down turn of agricultural production the rate of decline in poverty ratio was slow during 1980s but the public distribution system and anti-poverty programmes kept poverty from rising.

During 1990, poverty incidence dropped sharply but marginally increased in 1991-92 as a resultant effect of transition in economic management. During 1993-94 urban poverty dropped 6 percentage points while rural poverty declines 2.5 percentage points. Despite these successes over 310 million people were living in poverty in 1993-94.

Poverty in India remains predominantly rural, three out of every four persons live in rural areas. Changes in urban and rural poverty followed a similar path over most of the period during last 25 years with progress more rapid in rural area. By 1990 urban and rural poverty rates has nearly converged which has not been seen in other poor countries. In the early 1990s, poverty rose faster in rural than the urban areas but thereafter did not decline as rapidly.

The reduction in the poverty incidence that took place during the half century of the republic is uneven within the States and wide disparity exists across the States. In most cases better off States remained relatively affluent and reduced poverty while poorer States remained poor and made less progress in poverty reduction. At the same time, there are examples where poor States made major progress in poverty reduction and growth. In Kerala, for example, rural poverty declined at 2.4 per cent per annum between the early 1970s and early 1990s.

Other States where poverty incidence fell substantially during the period include West Bengal, Andhra Pradesh, Orissa and to a lesser extent, Gujarat and Tamil Nadu. Notably poor performers include Bihar and Uttar Pradesh. The better performer managed to reduce poverty at the rate of 1.5 per cent to 2.0 per cent per annum while poor performer rarely managed above 0.5 per cent per annum. Bihar, Madhya Pradesh and Uttar Pradesh have the highest concentration of poverty.

Three decades of experience over time and across the States suggests that the major factors in reducing poverty have been

(a) faster agricultural growth (as it raises agricultural wages and tends to depress the relative prices of food,
(b) lower inflation,
(c) infrastructure, and
(d) human resource development.

Most anti-poverty programmes seem to have had little sustained impact on poverty reduction, though they certainly eased the impact of the 1987 drought.[3]

Sustained decline in poverty in India began when its growth rate picked up from the 3.5 per cent rate that characterised in the early years. A decomposition of changes in poverty into a growth component (of a mean consumption) and a distribution component shows that the rise in growth in mean consumption accounts for 87 per cent of the cumulative decline in poverty and changes in distribution only 13 per cent.[4]

Different rates of agricultural growth and increase in rural wages were major factors which led to different levels as well as rates of decline of poverty across States. Green revolution technology, irrigation, and infrastructure were associated with rising rural wages and increased rural non-farm employment.[5] Growth in the urbanised part of the economy was less significant in reducing poverty across the States. The capital intensive import substituting nature of industrial development and its requirements for skilled rather than unskilled labour and labour market regulations limited the growth of formal sector employment. These factors limited the impact of urban growth on labour demand and kept the proportion of urban population relatively small.

Inflation hits the poor most as they doubly suffer. First, because of rise in the price of wage goods and second as their wages do not rise in proportion to rise in price level. Moreover, there is the traditional macroeconomic argument that the inflation hits the poor hardest because more of their assets are held in the form of currency.

In the mid-1990s growth increased sharply and human development indicators also improved, yet poverty rates, declined only marginally. Should the recent developments be taken as evidence that stabilisation and reforms go against the poor? I should argue yes. According to the Planning Commission, the growth rate of employment in the organised sector has declined from 1.44 per cent in 1991 to 0.44 in 1998. Based on the data up to 1993-94 an ILO economist has concluded in a recent study that the effective rate of unemployment was around 12 per cent and that the rate had not fallen despite the economy growing at a faster rate. The latest NSS data shows that situation has got even worse as non-agricultural employment in rural areas has registered an absolute decline and in urban areas the elasticity of employment is close to zero. Besides, there has been a big increase in casual labour and a fall in the labour force participation. That poverty reduction has been sluggish. In the early 1990s poverty worsened following the stabilisation of the macroeconomic policies followed earlier, a poor harvest and a decline in food availability. And it continued to worsen along with economic reform programmes. By 1993-94 it was somewhat below the 1987 level.

No doubt, India scored great success in reducing the incidence of poverty during 1970s and 1980s, but in the 1990s the fundamentals of growth both urban and rural are fading away. Neither the hi-tech industrialisation nor public investments in technology, rural and social infrastructure or prices are favourable to a dynamic growth in agriculture and the nonfarm economy that can simultaneously reduce poverty.

Challenges Ahead

"Over the past 50 years of our development as an independent nation, we can take justifiable pride in having successfully reversed the worst inequities of our colonial heritage and building a nation of considerable economic strength in a framework of democracy and federalism" says the Prime Minister Vajpayee in foreword to the Ninth Five-Year Plan 1997-2002. At the same time he reminds us, "We cannot, however, overlook our shortcomings or to the magnitude of challenges that lie ahead of us."[6]

The challenges lie ahead are more or less the same which we had inherited 50 years ago. Despite all achievements, one-third of people still live below poverty line and social indicators are still unacceptably low. The Ninth Five-Year Plan, therefore, marks a period of transition with a great hope to solve the tasks that lie ahead of us. "The time has come to redouble our efforts at development specially in the social and economic spheres, so that the country will realise its full economic potential and the poorest and the weakest will be able to shape their destiny in an unfeatured manner" to quote the plan document.[7]

"To fulfil the goal of growth with social justice and equity" the specific objectives of Ninth Five-Year Plan are

- (i) Priority to agriculture and rural development with a view to generating adequate productive employment and eradication of poverty.
- (ii) Accelerating the growth rate of economy with stable prices.
- (iii) Ensuring food and nutritional security for all, particularly the vulnerable sections of society.
- (iv) Providing the basic minimum services of safe drinking water, primary health care facilities, universal primary education, shelter and connectivity to all in a time bound manner.
- (v) Empowerment of women and socially disadvantaged groups.

How these objectives will be achieved is the greatest challenge before the nation. Despite impressive progress on economic fronts over the last 50 years, India is woefully lacking in providing basic services to the majority of people which alone can be effective to solve the problem of unemployment.

No doubt, India has grown economically over the years but it has not developed the real wealth of the nation, i.e., its people. The purpose of development is to create an enabling environment for people to enjoy long, healthy and creative lives. This simple but powerful truth has too often been forgotten in the pursuit of material and financial wealth.[8]

Development is not growth alone. It is growth plus change in value and institutions. Growth can provide material and financial wealth. A part of it can be used for development of the society. Development alone can be able to provide solution to the problem of poverty and unemployment. Creating an enabling environment for the people to live a long, health and creative lives is the biggest challenge for the country.

For the last 50 years we planned for development but worked for growth in the pursuit of material and financial wealth. The people were completely forgotten.

Why Poverty

Poverty results from the deprivation of an enabling environment for people to live long healthy and creative lives. Poverty is unacceptable deprivation in human well-being. It is the deprivation of their entitlement which has caused the poverty. The restoration of these entitlements be it social, political and economic—combined together will alone push them out of morass of poverty.

The Way Ahead

Social outcomes both embody poverty and represent a way out of poverty. Malnutrition, poor health, a lack of learning opportunities and limited choices are defining characterisation of poverty in India. Good education, health, nutrition and low fertility help reduce poverty by increasing opportunity to generate income. So also, an improved standard of living leads to gains in health and education, freeing people from the trap of ignorance and exposure to disease. Education empowers people to use information better to make better behavioural choice, healthy people are more likely to attend school or go to work and can learn and work more effectively. Unfortunately, the more common experience is that the costs of illness keep people in poverty and poor quality education limits their opportunity to escape poverty.

Progress in social sectors is both a vital yardstick of and a key element in the reduction of poverty. In spite of constitutional and often-stated government commitments for ensuring basic education and health services we have miles to go. No doubt, India has made substantial progress in education and health. Nevertheless, indicators continue to suggest surprisingly low levels of literacy and school enrolment and high level of infant mortality, maternal mortality relative to China and East Asian countries. Within the country inter and intra-State disparities are large. The poor rural women, disabled, and people belonging to SC and ST stand out as the most vulnerable sections of society. It would be difficult to reduce poverty substantially in the days ahead, without significant improvements in spending on and delivery of health and education services in the poverty concentrated States.

For the restoration of their entitlement to which the poor have been deprived earlier, the government must

(a) spend more effectively on elementary education and basic health system with better targeting for the poor and with more public funding to address the unfinished agenda.
(b) focus public education and health services on meeting consumer needs.
(c) realign the role of the State to focus on primary education and health.
(d) focus on meeting the holistic needs of the children.

Since majority of poor lives in rural area, an ambitious programmes combining policy and institutional reforms with a socially inclusive process of decentralisation can improve the quality of pubic spending in rural areas. Such a step can empower the poor, and liberalise the rural economy sequenced, inter-locking policy and institutional reform should:

(i) cut spending on input subsidies on irrigation, rural power and urea fertiliser, which benefit few while imposing increasingly serious distortions in agriculture and exploitation of natural resources.

(ii) spur reinvestment in more effective and equitable infrastructure in rural areas.

(iii) support the provision of more effective and equitable rural services, especially in health and education, technology generation and dissemination, and natural resources management.

(iv) empower the poor and socially disadvantaged improving their access to assets, health, education, safety nets and control over the institutions that deliver services in rural areas.

(v) reorient the rural financial system, making it an efficient market-oriented intermediary supporting private investment and mobilising the savings that will spur the growth of the rural economy.

(vi) adjust agricultural price policies on those influencing non-farm economy to encourage growth and private investment in agriculture and the non-farm economy, while safeguarding national and household food security objectives.

One of the most discussed issues in poverty reduction is the precise casual role of national per capita increase or of economic growth, in poverty outcomes for individual. Statistical studies in India and elsewhere have found a strong association between per capita income and poverty indicators, using both income and non-income measures of poverty. National poverty indicators such as the relationship between infant, mortality rates and per capita income, between ratio of female to male literacy and per capita national income and between average consumption and the incidence poverty, fall as per capita income rises. In this sense economic growth has been considered as the engine of poverty reduction. But it is an engine of poverty reduction if its distribution is equitable. In countries where most of poor live in rural areas, agricultural growth reduces poverty faster because it generates income for the poor and demand for goods and services that can easily be produced by poor. A cross country study of 35 developing countries estimates that a 10 per cent growth in agricultural GDP per capita leads to a 16 per cent increase in per capita income of bottom 20 per cent of population.[8] It finds that manufacturing growth reduces poverty directly by increasing the income of employed workers, but that it also worsens the distribution of income, reducing the effect on poor. Agricultural growth is not associated with worsening income distribution.

A growth pattern that results in a relatively higher expansion of low-skilled employment will show better result in poverty reduction. Inequality between income and non-income dimensions adversely affect poverty reduction programmes.

Globalisation and information technology have emerged as a new tool for faster growth. How to get private capital to flow to developing countries has emerged as an central issue. However, the Latin American and East Asian crisis have raised doubt over their impact on growth and poverty. The star performers in East Asia suffered severe setbacks in poverty reduction. In Indonesia as much as a decade's worth of progress have been wiped out in one step. Avoidance and management of such crises must clearly be part of any strategy for poverty alleviation in the first decade of 21st century.

Information technology continues to advance at a remarkable pace. The revolution will no doubt change the composition of economic activity toward what someone have called "The weightless economy". Though the potential for economic growth has greatly increased but still poverty among the poor will deny them to share the benefit of growth and it will increase inequality.

The key conclusion deduced from past experiences has been that:

> The countries that have been most successful in attacking poverty have encouraged a pattern of growth that makes efficient use of labour and have invested in the human capital of poor. The first provides the poor with opportunities to use their most abundant asset labour. The second improves their immediate well-being and increase their capacity to take advantage of the newly created possibilities. Together they can improve lives of the most poor in the world.[9]

NOTES AND REFERENCES

1. Human Development Report, UNDP, 1997, p. 15.
2. Between 1951 to 1997 the National Sample Survey Organisation (NSSO) has undertaker 38 National households surveys that have obtained reasonably sufficient comparable consumption expenditure information.
3. India: Policies to Reduce Poverty and Accelerate Sustainable Development, World Bank, 2000, p. 4.
4. Dutt, G., *Poverty in India and Indian States: An Update*, International Food Policy Research Institute, Washington D.C., 1997.
5. Punjab and Haryana had the highest GDP per capita up to the early 1990s and continue to be among the top 5 States in 1996-97.
6. Ninth Five-Year Plan 1997-2002, Vol. I, Government of India, Planning Commission.
7. *Human Development Report 1999*, UNDP, Oxford University Press, Delhi, p. 1.
8. Dutt, Gourav and Martin Ravallian, "Farm Productivity and Rural Poverty in India", *Journal of Development Studies*, UK, April 1998.
9. WDR, 1990, p. 51.

3

Understanding Poverty

Poverty is pronounced deprivation in well-being.[1] It is hunger, loneliness, nowhere to go when the day is over, deprivation, discrimination, abuse and illiteracy. It is the deprivation of lives that people can lead that poverty manifests itself. Poverty can involve not only the lack of well-being but the denial of opportunities and choices most basic to human development to lead a long, healthy creative life and to enjoy a decent standard of living, freedom, dignity, self-esteem and the respect of others.[2]

No doubt, the real wealth of a nation is its people and the purpose of development is to create an enabling environment for people to enjoy long, healthy and creative lives.[3] However, this simple and powerful truth is too after forgotten in the pursuit of material and financial wealth.

The last three decades of twentieth century saw great progress in reducing poverty and improving well-being in terms of increase in life expectancy, and decline in infant mortality rate and fertility rate. During the period life expectancy in the developing world increased 20 years on average, the infant mortality rate fall more than half and fertility rates declined almost half. In the past two decades, net primary school enrolment in developing countries increased by 13 per cent. Between 1965 and 1998 average incomes more than doubled in developing countries and during the last decade the number of people in extreme poverty fell by 78 million.

But in the beginning of 21st century poverty remains a global problem of huge dimension. Of the world's 6 billion people, 2.8 billion live on less than $2 a day and 1.2 billion on less than $1 a day. Six infants of every 100 do not see their first birthday and 8 do not survive to their fifth. Of those who do reach school age, 9 boys in 100 and 14 girls, do not go to primary school.

These macro trends conceal extraordinary diversity in experience across the world-large variations among regions, with some seeing advances and others setbacks, in crucial non-income measure of poverty. Widening inter and intra-regional disparities across the world have widen the horizon of deprivation and injustice making social mobility and equal opportunity alien for many.

Poverty means denial of opportunities and choices most basic to human development. Human development has been defined as the process of enlarging people's choices to lead a long and healthy life. The most critical choices are to be educated and to enjoy a decent standard of living.

Measuring Poverty

Over the years the concept of poverty has been defined in different ways. A person is poor if, and only if, his/her income level is below the defined poverty line. Poverty is also deprivation of material requirements for minimally acceptable fulfilment of human needs, including food. This concept of poverty goes well beyond the lack of income, it includes the need for basic health and education and essential services that have to be provided by the society to prevent people from falling into poverty. Poverty also represents the absence of same basic capabilities to function.

The above concepts of poverty have been based on income, basic needs and capability respectively. Whatever may be the concept of poverty, there are the people behind these statistics. Lifting them out of poverty will depend to a large extent on a better understanding of how many poor there are, where they live, and, above all, why they are poor. However, none of these definition turns out to be straightforward for understanding poverty. The concept should be more precise about what "poverty" really means.

Poverty is not the same as inequality. Whereas poverty is concerned with absolute standard of living of a section of people—the poor. Inequality refers to relative living standards across the whole society. Poverty, thus, could be defined as the inability to attain a minimal standard of living.[4] No doubt, to make this definition useful, few questions must be answered. How do we measure the standard of living? And having thus identified the poor, how do we express the overall severity of poverty in a single measure of index.

Measuring the Standard of Living

Per capita household incomes and expenditures have been considered as adequate yardsticks for the standard of living. But neither incomes nor expenditures, captures such dimensions of welfare as health, life expectancy, literacy and access to public goods or community resources. Being able to get clear drinking water public services to one's standard of living, it is not reflected in consumption or income as usually measured. Households with access to free public services are better off than those without, even though their incomes and expenditures may be the same.

Current consumption[5] reflects households, ability to better their standard of living through saving and borrowing despite fluctuating income. In this sense, consumption is a better measure of well-being than income.

Poverty is judged on the basis of certain norms. It becomes more important in the consumption-based measure of poverty. A consumption-based poverty line is comprising of two elements: first, the expenditure necessary to buy a minimum standard of nutrition and other basic necessities and second, an additional amount that varies from country to country, reflecting the cost of participating in everyday life of society. The former is relatively straightforward as the cost of minimum adequate intakes and other necessities can be calculated by looking at the prices of the foods that make up the diets of the poor. However, the later is for more subjective as in some countries indoor plumbing is a luxury, but in others it is necessity.

The perception of poverty has evolved overtime and varies widely from culture to culture. The criteria for distinguishing poor from non-poor often reflect specific national priorities and rights. In general, however, as they become wealthier, their perception of the minimum level of consumption changes.[6]

Once the poor has been distinguished from the non-poor, the simplest way to measure poverty is to express the number of the poor as proportion of the population. This method is known as headcount index though a useful measure, but often criticised on the ground that it ignores the extent to which the poor fall below the poverty line. The poverty gap criteria avoid this drawback. It measures the transfer that would bring the income of every poor person exactly up to the poverty line, thereby eliminating poverty. However, the headcount index and the poverty gap are insensitive to the extent of inequality among the poor. No doubt these measures often give a good indication of what has happened to poverty overtime, for many other purposes—including the effects of public policy on poverty—it is necessary to look carefully at the distribution of income below the poverty line.

Dimensions of Poverty

Poverty is caused not by lack of income alone but it is also caused by deprivation of most basic dimensions of human being: a long life, lack of basic education and access to public and private resources. This may be grouped into income and human dimensions of poverty. The multidimensionality of poverty raises the question of how to measure the overall poverty and how to compare achievements in its different dimensions. One dimension might move in a different direction from another. Health could improve while income worsens or an individual might be income poor but not health poor.

Using income or consumption has been a long tradition for identifying and measuring poverty. Based on the household income and expenditure surveys, the approach has become the workhouse of quantitative poverty analysis and policy discourse. It derives its strength from the fact that it is based on nationally representative samples and allows inferences about the conditions and evaluation of poverty at the national level. Though the approach makes it possible to obtain a broader picture of well-being and poverty, it is not problem free. It is often underestimate the severity of poverty. Household data cannot reveal inequality within household. In fact, this approach does not allow direct measurement of income or consumption poverty among women. A study that has disaggregated household consumption by individual members found that relying only on household information could lead to an understatement of inequality and poverty by more than 25 per cent.[7]

A key building block in developing income and consumption measure of poverty is the poverty line—the critical cut off in income or consumption below which an individual or household is determined to be poor. Since a universal line of poverty is not suitable for the analysis of poverty, many countries have constructed their own poverty lines reflecting the country's economic and social circumstances. After specifying the poverty line, the extent of poverty is assessed. The most straightforward way to measure poverty line is to calculate the percentage of the population with income or consumption level below the poverty line. This measure of poverty line is known as 'head-count' and the most commonly calculated measure of poverty. However, it fails to reflect the fact that among the poor people there may be wide differences in income levels of people located just below the poverty line.

Another poverty measure known as "Poverty Gap" take into account the distance of poor people from the poverty line and the degree of income inequality among the poor people.

Multi-Dimensionality of Poverty

Poverty cannot be measured in terms of income or expenditure alone in view of its various dimensions. Poverty is often caused by deprivation in any of the aspects for living a long healthy and creative life be it health, education, voice and power.

There are several possible approaches to aggregating measures of the different dimensions of poverty and well-being. Important among them are welfare function and composite index. A welfare function approach includes various dimensions of well-being and define poor people as all individuals below a specified minimum level of total welfare.[8]

This approach allows for trade off, using individuals, own choices for comparing situations and for assessing how much improvement is needed in one dimension to maintain welfare if another dimension worsens. However, this measure faces the difficulty of finding a suitable welfare function for comparisons between non-market elements of individual welfare. Choosing appropriate "weights" to form a single aggregate of these non-market elements of individual welfare from existing data has so far proved to be an insurmountable challenge.

Composite index is an answer to meet the challenge. There have been several well-known efforts in this direction, such as the physical quality of life index[9] and the human development index.[10] But, these indices do not provide correct number of poor people, another possibility is to count as poor everybody who is poor in anyone of the dimension of poverty. This method known as alternative aggression rules, adds value because it goes beyond income.

Global Patterns of Poverty

Of the world's 6 billion people, the 21st century begins with 1.2 billion people below poverty line.

This macro data conceal extraordinary diversity in different parts of the world. Between 1987-98 the share of population in developing and transition economies living on less than $1 a day fall from 28 per cent to 24 per cent as shown in Table 3.1. The number of people in poverty hardly changed.

As evidenced from Table 3.1 there are large regional variations in performance. There has been dramatic reduction in poverty in East Asia and Pacific, Middle East and North Africa.

TABLE 3.1: Share of Population Living on less than $1 a day

Region	1987	1990	1993	1996	1998
East Asia and Pacific	26.6	27.6	25.2	14.9	15.3
Excluding China	23.9	18.5	15.9	10.0	11.3
Europe and Central Asia	0.2	1.6	4.0	5.1	5.1
Latin America and the Caribbean	15.3	16.8	15.3	15.6	15.6
Middle East and North Africa	4.3	2.4	1.9	1.8	1.9
South Asia	44.9	44.0	42.4	42.3	40.0
Sub Sahara Africa	46.6	47.7	49.7	48.5	46.3
Total	28.3	29.0	28.1	24.5	24.0
Excluding China	28.5	28.1	27.7	27.0	26.2

Source: World Development Report, 2000.

TABLE 3.2: Income Poverty by Region

(in million)

Region	1987	1990	1993	1996	1998
East Asia and Pacific	417.6	452.4	431.9	265.1	278.3
Excluding China	114.1	92.0	93.5	55.1	65.1
Europe and Central Asia	1.1	7.1	18.3	23.8	24.0
Latin America and the Caribbean	63.7	73.8	70.8	76.0	78.2
Middle East and North Africa	9.3	5.7	5.0	5.0	5.5
South Asia	474.4	496.1	505.1	531.7	522.0
Sub Sahara Africa	217.2	242.3	273.3	289.0	290.0
Total	1183.2	1276.4	1304.3	1190.6	1198.9
Excluding China	879.8	915.8	955.9	980.5	985.7

Source: World Development Report, 2000.

But in other regions the number of people living on less than $1 a day has risen. In South Asia, the number of poor people rose over the decade from 474 million to 522 million (Table 3.2) even though the share of people in poverty fall from 45 per cent to 40 per cent. In Latin America and Caribbean the number of poor people rose by nearly 20 per cent. In Europe and Central Asia the number in poverty soared from 1.1 million to 24 million. In sub-Sahara Africa the number of poor people increased from a already high 217 million to 291 million over the same period.

These variations in regional performance also indicate a shift in the geographical distribution of poverty. In 1998 South Asia and sub-Sahara Africa accounted for around 70 per cent of the population living on less than $1 a day as against 60 per cent in 1967.

The poverty estimate in Tables 3.1 and 3.2 are based on poverty line that reflects what it means to be poorest countries. Table 3.3 represents estimates of poverty based on a combination of absolute and relative poverty concepts.

Though the poverty estimates in Tables 3.1, 3.2 and 3.3 are based on the same data and procedures, the effect of using relative poverty line instead of the $1 a day poverty line is that poverty becomes higher in regions with higher average consumption and also higher in regions with greater inequality. In Latin America, as evidenced from these tables, where nearly 15

TABLE 3.3: Relative Income Poverty by Region

Region	Regional average poverty line (1993 pp$ a day)	1987	1990	1993	1996	1998
East Asia and Pacific	1.3	33.0	33.7	29.8	19.0	19.6
Excluding China	1.9	45.1	38.7	30.8	23.2	24.6
Europe and Central Asia	2.7	7.5	16.2	25.3	26.1	25.6
Latin America and the Caribbean	3.3	50.2	51.5	51.1	52.0	51.4
Middle East and North Africa	1.8	18.9	14.5	13.6	11.4	10.8
South Asia	1.1	45.2	44.2	42.6	42.5	40.2
Sub-Sahara Africa	1.3	51.1	52.1	54.0	52.8	50.5
Total	1.6	36.3	37.4	36.7	32.8	32.1
Excluding China	1.8	39.3	39.5	39.3	38.1	37.0

Source: World Development Report, 2000.

per cent population was below the $1 a day poverty line, more population was below the relative poverty line. Similarly, in the Middle East and North Africa and in Europe and Central Asia poverty estimates are much higher by the relative poverty line. But the time trends remain unchanged.

Poverty Across Countries

There exists large variations in poverty performance across countries within each region. In Europe and Central Asia the proportion of the population living on less than $2 a day (at 1996 PPP) ranges from less than 5 per cent in Belarus, Bulgaria, Estonia, Hungary, Lithuania, Poland, and Ukraine to 19 per cent in Russia, 49 per cent in Kyrgyz Republic and 68 per cent in Tazikistan.[12] Among seven African countries during 1990s, Burkina Faso, Nigeria, Zambia and Zimbabwe experienced an increase in poverty, matching the regional pattern of the decade, while Ghana, Mauritania, and Uganda had declined.[13] In Latin American countries between 1989 and

1996, the incidence of poverty in Brazil, Chile, the Domininance Republic and Honduras declined and rose in Mexico and Republic Bolivariana de Venezuela.[14] The countries for which only urban surveys were conducted, poverty rose in Ecuador, stayed nearly unchanged in Uruguay and fell in Argentina, Bolivia, Colombia and Paraguay.

In East Asia poverty trends in the 1990s were influenced by the impact of the economic crisis. In Indonesia, the Republic of Korea, and Thailand, all suffered increases in poverty.[15] In Indonesia poverty increased from around 11 per cent in February 1996 to 18-20 per cent in February 1999. Though the poverty may declined considerably, it was higher than the pre-crisis level.[16] But, trends in China during 1996-98 were sensitive to the choice of welfare measure. Income poverty based on $1 a day declined continuously while saving in the rural areas increased substantially.

During 1990s, poverty reduction in South Asia also varied across countries. Despite its worst floods, poverty in Bangladesh declined but Pakistan and Sri Lanka made little or no progress in poverty reduction.[17] In India, there are divergent views on poverty reduction. Recent data from NSS surveys suggest that the pace of poverty reduction slowed during 1990s.

No doubt, country aggregates of different dimensions of poverty provide a useful overview of performance. But they hide as much as they reveal. There are distinct patterns of poverty within countries, and different groups within a country can become better or worse off. Poverty in various areas within a country can and does move in different directions. In Burkina Faso and Zambia rural poverty fell and urban poverty rose but the urban rise dominated, consequently total poverty rose. While aggregate poverty in Mexico, between 1989 and 1994 declined, there were large variations within the country. In China rapid income growth has been accompanied by increasing inequalities between rural and urban areas and among provisions.

Everywhere poverty tends to be associated with the distance from cities and the coast, as in China, Vietnam and Latin America. In China most of the poor reside in mountainous regions and townships. In Peru too, two-thirds of rural households in the poorest quintile are in the mountain regions, while fewer than a tenth are in the coastal region. In Thailand the incidence of poverty in the rural north-west was almost twice the national average in 1992.

Dimensions of human poverty are worse than the income poverty in many countries. Social indicators of development remain much worse for the income poor, than for the income non-poor. In Mali the difference in child mortality rates between the richest and poorest households is equal to the average gain in child mortality rate recorded over the last thirty years.[18] In South Africa the under five mortality rate for the poorest 20 per cent is twice as high as the rate for the richest 20 per cent, and three times as high in North-west and Southwest Brazil. The picture is the same for malnutrition. A study of 9 countries found that stunting[19] wasting [20] and being under-weight are higher among poor people in almost all countries.[21] However, the difference between poor and non-poor find to be smaller in countries with high average rates of malnutrition.[22]

The incidence of many illness, particularly communicable diseases is higher for poor people, while their access to health care is typically less. In India the prevalence of tuberculosis is more than four times as high in the poor fifth of the population as in the richest. And the prevalence of malaria more than three times as high.[23] Between 1992 and 1997 in 10 developing countries, only 41 per cent of the people suffering from acute respiratory infections were treated in health facility compared to 59 per cent of the non-poor. During the same period only 22 per cent of the births among the poorest 20 per cent of people were attended by medically trained staff compared to 76 per cent among the redust 20 per cent.[24]

Wide disparities also exist in access to schooling and in educational achievements. In some poor countries most children from the poorest households have no schooling at all. A study of Demographic and Health survey data found 12 countries in which more than half in 15-19 year old in the poorest 40 per cent households had zero years of schooling. These countries comprise of India, Pakistan, Bangladesh, Morocco and eight countries of Sub-Saharan Africa. In contrast, the median number of years completed by the people of same age group in the richest 20 per cent of households was 10 in India and 8 in Mexico. In other countries the gap in educational achievement was much smaller. It was one year in Kenya, two in Ghana and Tanzania and three in Indonesia and Uganda.[25]

Similar gap exists in primary enrolment rates. The rate for 6 to 14 year old is 52 percentage points lower for poorest households than for the richest households in Senegal, 36 percentage points lower in Zambia, and 19 percentage points lower in Ghana. The gaps are also large in North Africa and South Asia.

Within country differences in human development dimensions also exists between urban and rural areas, across regions, and across socio-economic classes. In China, there has been a widening rural urban gap in health status and health care use. While the rural population use of hospital services declined 10 per cent between 1985 and 1993, the urban population increased by 13 per cent.

One of the key factor influencing the variations in human dimensions of poverty within a country is the different achievement of women and men. The allocation of resources within households varies depending on the age and gender of the household member. However, estimating the number of poor men and women separately is difficult if not impossible, because consumption data are collected at the household level. Even so, available health and education data indicate that women are often disadvantaged. Large disparities also exist primarily caused by cast, ethnicity and indigenous status. Disadvantaged in many developed and developing countries, belong to minority casts, community, Scheduled Tribes, ethnic groups. They largely constitute the poor. The indigenous populations have much higher incidence of income poverty in a sample of Latin American countries for which data are available.[26]

Schooling attainments of these disadvantaged groups are also lower than for others groups. In Guatemala they have 1.8 years of schooling and the non-indigenous 4.9 years. In Peru indigenous people were 40 per cent more likely to be poor than those non-indigenous groups in 1994 and 50 per cent more likely in 1997. In rural Guatemala children of indigenous mother are more likely than those of non-indigenous mother to be stunted. In the inner cities of U.S.A. while married couples have an incidence of poverty of 5.3 per cent, while bulk of

Hispanic single mother households have an incidence of more than 45 per cent.

Evidences in India are no different from others. In India Scheduled Castes and Scheduled Tribes face a higher rise of poverty. Those are among structural poor who not only lack economic resources but whose poverty is closely linked to social identity, as determined mainly by cast. They have also worse human development indicators. Among rural Scheduled Caste women the literacy rate was 19 per cent in 1991, half that for the country and among Scheduled Caste men, 46 per cent compared to 64 per cent for the country. But, when several disadvantages are combined the situation becomes worse.

Volatility at the household level too influences the incidence of poverty. Studies of income poverty changes for the same household show significant movement in and out of poverty. While same groups are chronically below the poverty line, other groups face a high risks of falling into poverty. Some of the time studies for China, Ethiopia, Russia, and Zimbabwe find that the "always poor groups" is smaller than the "sometimes poor group".[27]

Factors causing chronic poverty varies from country to country. But, asset holding often play a key role. In China lack of physical capital is dominant in both chronic and transitory poverty, but household size and education of the head of household determine the likelihood of chronic poverty and not of transitory poverty.[28]

The analysis in the chapter indicates that the progress in income poverty reduction and human development varies widely across regions, countries and areas within countries. Much of the difference in performance across regions and countries can be attributed to differences in growth and development. In some of the countries poverty has been caused by collapses of growth and in some countries initial inequalities and pattern of growth caused poverty and account for the differences in poverty reduction in its multiple dimensions. In some cases initial differences include unequal access to assets, markets and infrastructure and uneven distribution of skills.

The differences in health and education among and within countries for example, also reflect the extent to which State institutions are responsive and accountable to poor people. In other cases social barriers linked with gender, the ethnicity, race and social status help perpetuate poverty and low levels of health and education among the socially disadvantaged. Policy basis against labour intensive sectors such as agriculture and small-scale manufacturing and skill basis technology result in lower reduction in income poverty.

The analysis in this chapter helps us in understanding poverty. It is amply clear that poverty goes beyond material deprivation and low levels of health and education. The inability to influence the decisions, that affect one's life, ill-treatment by State institutions and the bottlenecks caused by social barriers also caused poverty.

NOTES AND REFERENCES

1. World Development Report, 2000-2001, World Bank, Washington D.C., 2000, p. 15.
2. Human Development Report, UNDP, 1997, p. 15.
3. Human Development Report, UNDP, 1999, p. 1.
4. World Development Report, World Bank, 1990, p. 26.
5. Including consumption from own production.
6. For detail, see Sinha, Madhuri, *Poverty, Planning and Social Transformation*, 1993, Delhi, pp. 1-22.
7. Heddad Lawrence, and Revikanbur, 1990, "Are Better off Households More unequal or less unequal", Policy Research Working Paper No. 373, World Bank, Washington D.C.
8. Tsui, Kay Yuen, "Multidimensional Generalisation of the Relative and Absolute Indians", The Atkinson-Kolm-Sen Approved *Journal of Economic Theory*, Vol. 67, 1995, pp. 251-65.
9. Morris, David, *Measuring the Conditions of World's Poor: The Physical Quality of Life Index*, Oxford, Pergamon, 1979.
10. Human Development Report, UNDP, 1999.
11. Ravallion, Martin and Shaohua Chan, "What Can New Survey Data tell us about recent changes in Distribution and Poverty", *World Bank Economic Review*, 22(b), 1997, pp. 113-27.
12. Making Transition Work for Everyone: Poverty and Inequality in Europe and Central Asia, World Bank, Washington D.C., 2000.
13. Poverty Dynamics in Africa: An Update, World Bank, Washington D.C., 1999.
14. The World Bank, 2000, *op. cit.*, p. 25.
15. East Asia: Recovery and Beyond, The World Bank, Washington D.C., 2000.

16. The World Bank, 2000, *op. cit.*, p. 26.
17. "Poverty Trends and the Voice of the Poor", Poverty Reduction and Management Network, World Bank, 1999.
18. Bonilla-Chacin, Maria and Jaffrey S. Hammer, "Life and Death Among the Poorest", World Bank Development Research Group, Washington D.C., 1999.
19. Low height for age.
20. Low weight for age.
21. Wagestaff, Adam, The Health of the Poor Matters More: Child Survival Indicators in 9 Developing Countries, World Bank Human Development Network, 2000.
22. *Ibid.*
23. "Reducing Poverty in India: Portions for More Effective Public Services", World Bank, 1998.
24. World Bank, 1999, *op. cit.*
25. Filmer, Deon and Lant Pritchett, "Educational Enrolment and Attainment in India: Household Wealth, Gender, Village and State Effects", World Bank, Washington D.C., 1998.
26. Pracharopoulos, Adam and Harry Anthony Parrinos, "Indigenous People and Poverty in Latin America: An Empirical Analysis", World Bank, Washington D.C., 1994.
27. Baulach, Bob and John Hoddinott, "Economic Mobility and Poverty Dynamics in Developing Countries", Mimeograph 2000.
28. WDR 2000, p. 28.

4

The Factors that Caused Poverty

Formulating a two-part strategy for poverty alleviation, a decade ago, World Development Report stated:

> Countries that have been most successful in attacking poverty have encouraged a pattern of growth that make efficient use of labour and have invested in the human capital of the poor. Both elements are essential. The first provides the poor with opportunities to use their most abundant asset-labour. The second improved their immediate well-being and increases their capacity to take advantage of the newly created possibilities. Together they can improve the lives of the world's poor.[1]

From the above statement it can be deduced that countries who have failed to create an environment for its people to live a long, healthy and creative life are underdeveloped having large concentration of poor people. By not creating such an environment, poor people have been denied the choices and opportunities for living a tolerable life. In this sense poverty can mean more than a lack of what is necessary for material well-being. Poverty is caused not only by lack of income but also by the denial of opportunities and choices most basic to human development.

In the late twenties while replying to a set of questions at the instance of Mahatma Gandhi, Professor C.N. Vakil enumerated the following six causes for the poverty in India:

(i) Not enough work for the vast masses of the agricultural population during the off season;

(ii) The social system which imposes the burden upon one person of supporting a large family;
(iii) The presence of a large number of able-bodied beggars;
(iv) Enervating climate;
(v) Resignation to fate and consequent want of determination;
(vi) Faulty education system.

"While these are contradictory causes of more or less value" said Mahatma Gandhi reacting upon these answers, "With the exception of the first non-seems to me to go to the root of the matter. There is no doubt that the foreign exploitation of India is a cause of poverty. This exploitation is a hydra-headed monster taking a variety of shapes to suit given occasions. The poverty of India will never be removed as long as exploitation continues unabated. Even the spinning wheel or any other subsidiary occupation that may be provided for the millions of peasantry will bring only partial relief. He, therefore, who would explore the remedies for removing poverty has to tackle first the question of stopping the continues drain."[2]

Continued drain from India to England was considered the prime cause of poverty by Mahatma Gandhi. Yet, fifty years after Independence the problems of poverty remain abated. For the people of India stepped in abysmal poverty and ignorance, the attainment of independence was only the first step towards creating an environment for the people to live a long, healthy and creative life. Throughout the struggle for freedom a promise was made to the people for creating such an environment once independence is achieved.

For creating an environment for the people to fulfil their cherished goal India followed the path of planned development. But contrary to the expectation of many such an environment was never created.

Successive Five-Year Plans followed the avoid objective of removal of poverty but so far this has not been achieved, the prevalence of poverty, virtually unchanged during the years, can be seen most clearly in the conditions of life of the two disadvantaged groups of Indian society: the Scheduled Castes and Scheduled Tribes. The social disabilities from which large number of Harijans continue to suffer in many parts of the country are in a large part related with their economic statues and the lack of bargaining power which makes their role as landless agricultural workers in a situation of overall labour surplus. For growth to have some meaning, a part of it must be used for development of the society in terms of health, education and increase in economic and social status of the poor.

Factors that Caused Poverty

Poverty is caused, as the poor has not been ensured to participate in and contribute to growth which requires the adoption of appropriate national and sectoral policies and measures to help the poor group new income earning opportunities. The pattern of growth that increases the efficient use of assets owned by the poor does not exist nor the access of the poor to land, credit, infrastructure and productive inputs exists. Investment in human capital, which is critical for enabling the poor to seize opportunities, does not take place. Thus poverty is caused both by lack of physical as well as human capital.

Most of the poor in developing countries depend on income from their labour as wage-earner or self-employed. The countries that have failed to create such avenues for the poor to get their income are poor both in terms of growth and development. The poor are unable to participate in the growth as they lack assets nor their human faculties have been developed, lack of rural development and urban employment often enhances the poverty of the poor.

Successful rural development provides strong support for infrastructural development and makes technical innovations accessible for small and marginal formers. And a rising urban demand for labour in industry and services plays an increasing role as income rise. Such an environment has never been created in poor developing countries, although their economy are predominantly rural and agricultural.

The expansion of agriculture is the driving force behind rural development which in turn lays the foundation for broadly-based poverty reducing growth. The poor benefit directly, if they are farmers and they benefit indirectly from growth in demand for firm labour and for the products of the rural non-firm sector. Evidences suggest that in agriculturally predominant countries there is a strong association between growth in agricultural purchasing power and real wages.[3] Besides agricultural growth helps the rest of the economy, countries with rapid agricultural growth have also had rapid industrial growth.[4] Neglect of agriculture in agriculturally predominant economy is the root cause of poverty.

Stagnated urban employment and wages in urban sector cause poverty to rise as these are broad determinants of the pace of poverty. Most studies have found that people migrate mainly for economic reasons. Poverty both absolute and relative and income variability, which leads to greater vulnerability, cause people to move.

Labour market policies for the organised sector are usually intended to raise welfare or reduce exploitation. Inadequate labour market policies is a cause for urban poverty. In most of the developing countries, the informal sector too plays a prominent role in providing employment and incomes. Lack of appropriate policy for the informal sector breads poverty in cities and towns. The informal sector is very diverse in its income structure and activities. It is dominated by one person firm and small-scale entrepreneurs that employ a few apprentices and hired labour. But preferential treatment for large firms has undermined the informal sector leading to poverty of the people.

Inadequate urban infrastructure also breads poverty. Growth that creates impact on the poor have a greater impact on the poor if they have access to land, credit and public infrastructure and services. Similar is the case with rural infrastructure. Poor have less access to public infrastructure than prosperous.

Poor Delivery of Social Services

Poverty is caused by less investment in human capital. Inadequate facilities for education, health and nutrition produce worst consequences for the poor. History is replete with examples that investing in human capital often attacks some of the most important causes of poverty.

During the last four decades there have been tremendous

progress in social indicators in the developing countries as a whole. But the advances have been uneven among regions and among socio-economic groups within countries. Progress in the social sectors requires a long-term commitment for making education, health care and other social services accessible to all sections of society. Where that commitment is lacking and where government policies have failed to reach the poor, social needs remain staggeringly high. There is overwhelming evidence that human capital is one of the keys for reducing poverty. Moreover, improvements in health, education, and nutrition reinforce each other. However, the poor generally lack access to basic services. There is too little investment in the human capital and this increases the probability that they and their children will remain poor.

The principal asset of the poor is labour time. Education increases the productivity of this asset. The result at the individual level is higher income. There is a strong link between education and growth. The effectiveness of education as a weapon in the fight against poverty goes well beyond productivity in the labour market. One year of mother's education has been associated with 1 per cent decrease in under 5 mortality. The children of better educated mothers, other things being equal, tend to be healthier.

However, the effect of better health and nutrition on productivity is less well documented than the effect of education. But it has its own role, with better health and nutrition productivity increases.

Rapid population growth is also an important cause of poverty. Poverty and rapid population growth reinforce each other in a number of ways. Low wages, inadequate education and high infant mortality all linked to poverty-contribute to high fertility and thus to rapid population growth. The link leading from poverty to high fertility is well established. Providing the poor with access to social services requires a clear commitment which is often lacking in most of the developing countries. Much can be learned from decades of experience in countries at different level of development and with varying needs. But none is interested to learn from history and to provide the services that the poor need most and to make the existing services more effective.

Inadequate Safety Nets

Not all the poor benefit from the policies discussed earlier to go out of poverty trap in the short-run to fully participate and the old and disabled never participate. Even those who benefits from these policies, there are a few who are vulnerable to adverse events. These people need some help to face such situations. The first group can best be helped through a system of income transfers and the second group requires a safety net in the form of income insurance to help people through short-term stress and calamities. Safety nets in the form of food pricing and distribution, public employment schemes and social securely—are needed when their survival is threatened.

Individuals, families and communities have ways of coping with poverty. Individuals and families redistribute and stabilise consumption, diversity income sources, migrate and give and receive transfers. But many of the poor are inadequately protected by these strategies. There are limits to what those who are unable to work can do to protect themselves and limit to households looking after them can do to raise household income to tolerable levels. Poor, vulnerable households, on the margins of subsistence at the best of times, are hard pressed to protect themselves in the face of series of shocks. And the effectiveness of community insurance depends crucially on the extent to which local incomes are affected simultaneously. Unanticipated shocks such as severe agricultural fluctuations, deterioration in terms of trade and famines are creating hardship every year for the poor.

The State therefore has a role in aiding households and communities in times of insecurity and insuring minimum levels of provision to those unable to gain from the growth process. Effective policies would take into account what individuals and households could do to protect themselves and what there limitations are. Government interventions should also try to involve people in the solutions rather than treat them as passive recipients of relief.

The countries who have made provisions of safety nets for those people are moving towards solutions. Some of them who have taken into the cost-effectiveness of these measures are moving faster in this direction. The cost-effectiveness is the budgetary cost of delivering a given amount of benefit. Benefits usually change the way the poor and others behave and this affects cost-effectiveness.

Absence of transfers and safety nets for these groups in need of special assistance may be temporarily in danger when events take an unfavourable turn. The first group need a system of transfers that would ensure an adequate standard of living. The second group would be saved by variety of safety nets. However, because of economic, political, social and cultural reasons, such programmes have either remained as vote catching device or implemented in a way that has benefited well to do segments of the society. Consequently poor derived little benefit from these transfers and safety nets.

Most of the people in developing countries live in rural areas and it is there that the need for effective transfers and safety nets is greatest. No doubt, well-designed rural public employment schemes can provide insurance against a risky agricultural environment. The key to such schemes, success is to reaching the poor. But, it has hardly happened.

Neglect of the infrastructure to provide widespread access to basic nutrition, health and sanitation service has provided fuel in the fire. Its absence has aggravated poverty.

Economic Reforms and the Poor

Stabilisation and structural adjustment under economic reforms programme, launched a decade ago, have adversely affected the poor and the poverty is on increase. When structural adjustment issues came to the fore, little attention was paid to its effects on the poor. Macroeconomic issues seemed more pressing and many expected that there would be a rapid transition to new growth paths. In the beginning macroeconomic recovery and structural change were slow in coming. Evidences of declines in income and cut back in social services began to mount. This have attracted the attention of governments and funding agencies including the World Bank to study the effects on poor and suggesting specific measures to protect the interest of the poor.

The starting point for macroeconomic adjustment was macroeconomic disequilibrium whether the causes were external or internal, the system everywhere was an unsustainable current account deficit internal financial problems, often linked with inflation and slow growth. Everywhere, adjustment is having two objectives, reducing the demand for imports and domestic goods to stabilise economic conditions and restructuring the economy to reach a better growth tract. Many policies such as exchange rate and fiscal measure could have both demand reducing and restructuring effects.

Though it was hoped that the effects on the poor of demand reducing and restructuring policies would be positive in the long-run as it aimed for a more efficient use of labour. Experiences suggest that it could not happened in countries who went either for industrial or agricultural policy restructuring. In this short-run it created difficulties for two reasons. First, because the process of restructuring was often sluggish and uneven. Firms and labour markets took time to adjust, and in the meantime economics suffered higher unemployment or underemployment and labour income declined. Second, demand reducing measures were unavoidable for controlling inflation and reducing fiscal deficit, these hurt the poor and non-poor alike. The need for cuts in public spending adversely affected delivering social services and providing transfers and safety nets.

Effective adjustment can ease the burden on the poor in the short-run and reduce poverty in the long-run. Yet adjustment possess dilemmas for political leaders. The policies often impose costs on constituents, when monopoly profits or transfers are cut. They also involve a trade off between present and future, a trade off that politicians, with election to win, interest group to satisfy, and coups to deflect, find awkward.

The success of adjustment measures depend on the feasibility of building conditions of those who benefit and on careful sequencing with respect to political as well as economic objectives. Favourable initial conditions reduce the political as well as the economic costs of adjustment. However, severe imbalances and large external shocks increase the temptation to delay adjustment. If people think that economic difficulties are externally caused and adjustment policies extremely imposed, there is a high risk of losing political support. Weak or divided governments and those facing electoral challenges are likely to procrastinate.

Where the new economic teams have come to power and the policies of the previous team have been discredited, there is scope for ambitious reform. In such cases technically and economically feasible demand reducing and restructuring measures should be introduced as quickly as possible. Swift actions establishes the creditability of the programme, limit the opportunity for resistance and increases the likelihood that new leader will reap the fruits of reform.

A mix of swift action on the fundamentals and efforts to cushion consumption is often justified on welfare grounds. The political case for this approach is also strong. But there is an important difference between the two rationale. Concern with welfare puts the emphasis on the poor, whereas the preoccupation with politics points the other way, dictating that losses among powerful groups be moderated. In this process the poor suffer most and poverty increases. The expected benefit in the long-run is too long and generations have to wait for the benefit.

Conflicts between political imperatives and the goal of reducing poverty are common. This is especially true when demand reducing measures are required or when growth promoting policies help the rural poor but hurt the towns. In any case help to losers in the short-run play a crucial political role.

The experiences so far suggests that efforts to restructure economies in the wake of a macro-economic crisis are, by and large, consistent with a medium-term shift toward a pattern of growth and human capital formation that would reduce poverty. In the short-run, however, some of the poor are the greatest loser as a result of shifts in the pattern of public spending toward goods and services consumed by the poor.

In developing countries absence of efficient labour intensive growth based on appropriate market incentives, physical infrastructure, institutions, and technological innovation on the one hand and inadequate provision of social services including primary education, basic health care and rising population have been important factors that have caused poverty to rise, apart from lack of income generating assets and avenues.

NOTES AND REFERENCES

1. The World Development Report, World Bank, 1990, p. 51.
2. Sinha, R.K., "Poverty and Planning" in *Economic Development: Planning and Policy in India*, Vol. 5, Deep and Deep Publications, New Delhi, 1989, p. 285.
3. See World Bank, World Development Report, 1990, p. 71.
4. See World Bank, World Development Report, 1986.

5

Poverty Reduction: Progress and Challenges

Since Independence, India has accorded great importance to poverty reduction. Poverty reduction has been a major goal of all Five-Year Plans. The opening paragraph of First Five-Year Plan states:

> The central objectives of planning in India is to raise the living standard of the people and to open to them opportunities for a richer and varied life. Planning must therefore, aim both at utilising more effectively the resources, human and material available to the community so as to obtain from them a larger output of goods and services, equalities of income, wealth and opportunity. A programme aiming only at raising output might result in most of the increased wealth flowing into the hands of a few, leaving the masses of the people in this present state of poverty.[1]

To measure its success in achieving the goal the government commissioned a series of household surveys on poverty, which began in 1951. These survey provide an unparalleled record of national efforts to reduce poverty.[2] Since 1970s the percentage of population living below poverty line has been reduced but progress has been uneven overtime and across States and the number of poor continued to rise.

The Ninth Five-Year Plan which was launched in the 50th year of Independence while taking stock of the success of planning process as well as its failure to provide appropriate direction for the socio-economic development of the country stated to "usher in a new era of people-oriented planning in which not only the government at the Centre and States, but the people at large, particularly the poor can fully participate".[3]

Such an affirmation of the goal became inevitable since faster growth failed to reduce poverty as it should have nor it created the high quality of jobs needed to satisfy the aspiration of increasingly educated youth. Growth was uneven and low level of social development today has become a major constraints.[4]

The objectives and strategy of the Ninth Five-Year Plan have been formulated mainly for enhancing the quality of life of the people, generation of productive employment and regional balance. No development process can be sustainable unless it leads to visible and widespread improvement in these areas. To help achieve this, the Ninth Five-Year Plan has some of its objective[5] as

(i) Priority to agriculture and rural development, with a view to generating productive employment and eradication of poverty.
(ii) Enhancing food and nutritional security for all, particularly the vulnerable section of society.
(iii) Providing the basic minimum services of safe drinking water, primary health care facilities. Universal primary education, shelter and connectivity to all in a time bound manner.
(iv) Empowerment of women and socially disadvantaged groups as agents of socio-economic change and development.

There is hardly any difference between the objectives of the First Five-Year Plan and the Ninth Five-Year Plan. Removal of poverty and attainment of full employment have been the avoid objective of Five-Year Plans yet after 50 years the problems have been continuing unabated.

The Performance

The profile of the poverty during the last 50 years can be seen in Table 5.1. From the early 1950s to the mid 1970s, poverty rate fluctuated without a clear trend. During 1951-55, the average headcount index of poverty was 53 per cent, about the same as in 1973-74. From 1973-74 to the mid-1980s, poverty incidence declined fairly steadily from 54 per cent in 1986-87, a decline of about 2 per cent per annum. However, poverty reduction slowed in the late 1980s, mainly because of poor weather conditions, and the resultant down turn in agricultural production. The public distribution system (PDS) and anti-poverty programmes kept poverty from rising as it had in such circumstances in the past. Poverty incidence declined rapidly in 1990 but could not be sustained. In 1991-92, a transitory worsening of poverty incidence occurred with the balance of payment crisis, decline in growth and impact of stabilisation. Besides, it was also related to factors like poor harvests, limited agricultural imports and large agricultural procurement. These factors kept food prices high. By 1993-94 the incidence of poverty declined to 35 per cent.

In fact, the decline of poverty was not simply a process whereby a segment of the population which had previously been located just below the poverty line was able to lift itself above the line, while the remaining poor left unaffected. Rather it also improved the consumption of those far below the poverty line. Despite these successes, over 310 million people were living in poverty in 1973-74, 50 per cent more than the poor in Sub-Saharan Africa. During the same period, some comparator countries were successful in reducing poverty. Indonesia reduced poverty from 70 per cent range in the early 1970s, to below 10 per cent in the early 1990s. Even after the East Asian crisis, its poverty may still less than 20 per cent.[7]

No doubt, Indian poverty remains predominantly rural. Three of every four poor live in rural areas. Changes in urban and rural poverty followed a similar path over most of the last quarter of 20th century, with more progress in rural areas during 1970s, and 1980s. By 1990, urban and rural poverty rates had nearly converged. In the early 1990s, poverty rose faster in rural areas and thereafter did not decline rapidly.

A wide disparity in poverty across States and their uneven progress in poverty reduction has been a key feature of the evolution of poverty in India. In most cases better off States remained relatively affluent and reduced poverty, while poor States remained poor and made little progress in poverty reduction. India's pervasive poverty, predominantly rural is mirrored

TABLE 5.1: Poverty in India 1951-97 (with correction for CPIAL)
(Poverty line = Rs. 49 per capita per month at Oct. 1973-Jun. 1974 rural prices)

NSS Survey period	Headcount index			Poverty gap index			Squared poverty gap index		
	Rural	Urban	National	Rural	Urban	National	Rural	Urban	National
3. Aug. 1951–Nov. 1952	47.37	35.46	45.31	16.05	11.14	15.20	7.53	4.82	7.06
4. Apr. 1952–Sep. 1952	43.87	36.71	42.63	14.64	10.91	13.99	6.71	4.41	6.31
5. Dec.1952–Mar.1953	48.21	40.14	46.80	16.29	13.25	15.76	7.56	5.96	7.28
6. May 1953–Sep.1953	54.13	42.77	52.15	19.03	13.83	18.12	9.12	6.29	8.62
7. Oct. 1953–Mar 1954	61.29	49.92	59.30	21.95	17.24	21.12	10.26	7.74	9.82
8. Jul. 1954–Mar. 1955	64.24	46.19	61.07	25.04	15.76	23.41	12.50	7.02	11.54
9. May 1955–Nov. 1955	51.83	43.92	50.44	18.44	14.65	17.78	8.80	6.40	8.38
10. Dec. 1955–May 1956	48.34	43.15	47.43	15.65	13.34	15.24	6.71	5.41	6.48
11. Aug. 1956–Feb 1957	58.86	51.45	57.55	19.45	18.16	19.22	8.50	8.51	8.50
12. Mar. 1957–Aug. 1957	62.11	48.88	59.77	21.69	16.31	20.73	10.01	7.25	9.52
13. Sep. 1957–May 1958	55.16	47.75	53.84	19.01	15.95	18.47	8.78	7.00	8.46
14. Jul. 1958–Jun 1959	53.26	44.76	51.75	17.74	13.75	17.03	7.88	5.87	7.52
15. Jul. 1959–Jun 1960	50.89	49.17	50.58	15.29	15.83	15.39	6.13	6.75	6.24
16. Jul 1960–Aug. 1961	45.40	44.65	45.27	13.60	13.84	13.64	5.53	5.83	5.59
17. Sep. 1961–Jul. 1962	47.20	43.55	46.54	13.60	13.79	13.64	5.31	6.05	5.45
18. Feb. 1963–Jan 1964	48.55	44.83	47.85	13.88	13.29	13.77	5.49	5.17	5.43
19. Jul. 1964–Jun. 1965	53.66	48.78	52.75	16.08	15.24	15.93	6.60	6.38	6.56
20. Jul. 1965–Jun. 1966	57.60	52.90	56.71	17.97	16.82	17.75	7.60	6.98	7.49

21.	Jul. 1966–Jun. 1967	64.30	52.24	62.00	22.01	16.81	21.02	10.01	7.19	9.47
22.	Jul. 1967–Jun. 1968	63.67	52.91	61.60	21.80	16.93	20.86	9.85	7.22	9.35
23.	Jul. 1968–Jun. 1969	59.00	49.29	57.11	18.96	15.54	18.29	8.17	6.54	7.85
24.	Jul. 1969–Jun. 1970	57.61	47.16	55.56	18.24	14.32	17.47	7.73	5.86	7.36
25.	Jul. 1970–Jun 1971	54.84	44.98	52.88	16.55	13.35	15.91	6.80	5.35	6.51
27.	Oct. 1972–Sep.1973	55.36	45.67	53.37	17.35	13.46	16.55	7.33	5.26	6.90
28.	Oct. 1973–Jun. 1971	55.72	47.96	54.10	17.18	13.60	16.43	7.13	5.22	6.73
32.	Jul. 1977–Jun. 1978	50.60	40.50	48.36	15.03	11.69	14.28	6.06	4.53	5.72
38.	Jan. 1983–Dec. 1983	45.31	35.65	43.00	12.65	9.52	11.90	4.84	3.56	4.53
42.	Jul. 1986–Jun. 1987	38.81	34.29	37.69	10.01	9.10	9.79	3.70	3.40	3.63
43.	Jul. 1987–Jun. 1988	39.23	36.20	38.47	9.28	9.12	9.24	2.98	3.06	3.00
44.	Jul. 1988–Jun. 1989	39.06	36.60	38.44	9.50	9.54	9.51	3.29	3.29	3.29
45.	Jul. 1989–Jun. 1990	34.30	33.40	34.07	7.80	8.51	7.98	2.58	3.04	2.69
46.	Jul. 1990–Jun. 1991	36.43	32.76	35.49	8.64	8.51	8.61	2.93	3.12	2.98
47.	Jul. 1991–Dec. 1991	37.42	33.23	36.34	8.29	8.24	8.28	2.68	2.90	2.74
48.	Jan 1992–Dec. 1992	43.47	33.73	40.93	10.88	8.82	10.35	3.81	3.19	3.65
50.	Jul. 1993–Jun. 1994	36.66	30.51	35.04	8.39	7.41	8.13	2.79	2.42	2.69
51.	Jul. 1994–Jun. 1995	39.75	33.50	38.40	8.89	8.38	–	2.90	2.80	–
52.	Jul. 1995–Jun. 1996	37.46	28.04	35.00	8.31	6.78	–	2.64	2.22	–
53.	Jan 1997–Dec. 1997	35.69	29.99	34.40	8.39	7.77	–	2.83	2.73	–

Note: All poverty measures are expressed as percentage.

Source: Datta (1997 and 1999)

in health, education and nutrition indicators that remain too low. Although infant mortality rates, fell from 146 deaths per thousand births in 1950s at the end of 1990s, it is one of the highest in the world. Life expectancy at birth increased to 60 years at the end of 1990s, that of twice in 1947 was below that of China which was 69 years. In 1993-94 adult literacy rates ranging from 42.8 per cent to 49 per cent were recorded in Bihar, U.P., Rajasthan, Madhya Pradesh and A.P. and female literacy rates were much lower. It was 25.6 per cent in Rajasthan, 26.3 in Bihar, 29.7 per cent in U.P.

Sharp disparities remain between development-oriented States and laggard between men and women, between adult and children and between urban and rural areas.

TABLE 5.2: Poverty in India: 1993-94
(Estimates based on the expert group methodology)

	Rural	Urban	Total
Head count	37.1	33.2	361.0
Number of Poor (in million)	244.0	76.0	320.0
Per cent of total	76.3	23.7	100.0
Poverty gap	8.4	8.4	8.4
Squared Poverty gap	2.8	3.1	2.9

Source: Haque, Lanjouw and Ravallion 1998.

The range in poverty reduction among the States is very wide. Kerala's progress in reducing poverty by 2.4 per cent per year on average between 1957-58 and 1993-94 outpaced Bihar by more than 120 times and Rajasthan by more than four times. Kerala is the top performer overall among the 16 major States which together accounted for more than 97 per cent of India's population in 1991.

While the relative position of a State as evidenced in Table 5.3 is rarely identical across different indicators of well-being, certain regularities appear across the columns of table. Bihar Orissa, Uttar Pradesh, Madhya Pradesh, Rajasthan and to some extent Andhra Pradesh are nearly always clustered at the low end of the ranking. These States account for nearly half of the country's population. By contrast, Kerala, Punjab and Haryana having less than 7 per cent of country's population

TABLE 5.3: Alternative Indicators of well-being Ranking of States, 1993-94

Survey period	Headcount Index			Life Expectancy		Infant Mortality	Literacy Ratio	
	Total	Rural	Urban	M	F		M	F
Punjab	16	16	16	13	12	14	8	11
Andhra Pradesh	15	15	14	14	7	8	2	5
Gujarat	14	14	15	15	6	10	11	9
Kerala	13	11	10	10	14	15	16	16
Haryana	12	13	12	12	11	7	9	8
Rajasthan	11	10	11	11	4	4	4	1
Himachal Pradesh	10	12	13	13	–	–	14	14
Karnataka	9	7	7	7	10	9	7	7
Tamil Nadu	8	6	6	6	9	12	12	12
Maharashtra	7	5	4	4	12	13	15	13
West Bengal	6	9	8	8	8	11	10	10
Assam	5	8	9	9	–	5	13	15
U.P.	4	4	5	5	2	3	3	3
M.P.	3	3	3	3	1	2	5	4
Orissa	2	2	1	1	3	1	6	6
Bihar	1	1	1	1	5	6	1	2

Source: As per Table 5.2, Economic Survey 1996-97.

cluster near the top for most indicators.

Even within States, because of wide geographic variation, the relative positions is rarely identical across all the regions of a State. Of the 10 poorest regions in 1993-94 as in 1987-88 four were either in Bihar or Orissa. Inequality is also high within the regions of the richer States.

More than geographic differences in poverty reduction and regional inequality more noticeable are the inequities that persist across gender, caste and ethnic groups. 80 per cent of girls from households of the top 20 per cent of population complete the 8 years of basic education, only 9.5 per cent from poorest 40 per cent while members of the Scheduled Castes, particularly their children are more likely to die prematurely.[8]

These differences reflect more than natural advantages or disadvantages. In fact, they mirror conscious decisions, in the case of Kerala, to invest in the poor, especially in improving their health and education and consequently, their opportunity to gain a share of economic progress. Having foregone such investment, Bihar, the poorest States among 16 major States, has the fifth lowest level of male literacy, the second lowest level of female literacy and sixth highest level of infant mortality. Kerala by contrast (Table 5.3) has the lowest infant mortality rate and the highest rate of female and male literacy.

Who are the Poor in India?

Poverty in India does not wear a uniform face. Primarily it is rural in its nature and spreads to urban areas in search of employment opportunities. Many of the poor manage to provide a steady subsistence level of income for themselves and their families. Others, truly, are often without any means of livelihood. Most gained their low socio-economic status as an inheritance and remain prisoners of it because they own little or no land, few productive assets, no knowledge of reading or writing and ill-nourished bodies which make them prey to frequent illness. At higher average risk are illiterate rural women, members of the Scheduled Tribes or Castes of a landless households.

Primarily poverty in India is rural. A typical poor household in rural area is one at the low end of the cast hierarchy.

More often they are the members of the Scheduled Castes or Scheduled Tribes. Landlessness in terms of lack of access to fertile, well-watered agricultural land has been a cause and characteristic of poverty in every village. In the regions with high tribal population, the very poor are often characterised as those who spend most of the year relying on gathering and selling firewood or folder for their livelihood. The women and children of these households are often the primary collectors of this products. Contributing in this way to household subsistence deprives their children of educational opportunities that would equip them to break the cycle of poverty.

Social stratification, based on castes, ethnicity, and gender are impediments of the mobility of the poor. The unprivileged of the society are easily distinguishable from the rest of the society in terms of both their very low material well-being and their limited opportunities to improve their well-being.

Rural labour market imperfections have seriously weakened the force of the non-firm sector in reducing poverty.[9]

Escaping Poverty: Impediments of the Way

Lack of non-firm employment, access to land, enthusiasm for primary universal education and health care facilities are the most important barriers on the path of escaping poverty.

States which accounts for large number of poor are having rural poverty. Most of such poor consider non-farm employment as route to upward mobility. However, finding of a World Bank study indicates that the poor are not generally well placed to take advantage of non-farm employment, which would lead to better lives. In general, however, it has been observed, upward mobility usually occurs when a family members finds employment in some regular, salaried, non-agricultural occupation.

With the gradual transformation of the rural economy, rural elites have become more interested in non-agricultural source of income. Consequently, the poor now facing stiffer competition for those non-agricultural sources of income which are available.[10]

In some of the States poor households in other backward classes have begun to move up the economic ladder, through shifts to cash crops or animal husbandry. However, this is more an exception than the rule as access to land is out of the reach of the rest of the poor landless households.

Little enthusiasm for education in the past has become a hindrance for the poor. The economic and social benefits of education are greatest when a critical minimum level of educational attainment has been achieved across the population. Universal primary education would have high pay-offs in economic and social benefits. The benefits of education extend beyond individuals who receive schooling directly. Others in the society also gain. The resulting improvements in economic efficiency provide continuing justification for public sector involvement in education.

The economic outcomes of education are on higher scale. Aggregate production functions suggest that one year increase in the average education of workforce can raise output by 13 per cent and that the increased educational level can contribute around one quarter of increase in output. Firm based production functions show that in agriculture, education helps increase primarily by adoption of new technologies and firming fractions. Another study also suggests that private social returns to education are around 6-9 per cent with the highest returns registered for low-cast graduates.[10]

Eradicating Poverty: The Available Options

Growth and development enhancing public policies are the *sine qua non* of lasting progress in reducing poverty. Everywhere the strongest inputs to poverty alleviation has come from economic growth. Economic growth widens economic opportunities, provides the resources needed to invest in human development and creates the very foundation that would increase its returns and create an environment for the people to live a long, healthy and creative life.

India's overarching development objective in the beginning of this millennium has been growth with equity. For this to happen, the country hope to achieve and sustain annual growth of 7-8 per cent that would largely benefit the poor.

The rapid growth of the last decade has shown how much the country and the poor stand to gain from a more market-oriented development strategy. The strong economic performance has helped build support across national political spectrum for the liberalisation of the economy. At what speed this will be pursued remains, however, unresolved—yet critical—issue. The pace will determine the country's performance and the potential for poverty reduction.

Development of the last decade should not be taken as evidence that stabilisation and reforms have worked against poor. We would argue not because of the fact it has resulted in reduction in urban poverty. More importantly the issue is not reforms and stabilisation, which were badly needed to correct an unsustainable economic situations, but incomplete and partial reforms. In particular, it is generally agreed that agriculture, which remains less reformed and most distorted sector, lost its impetus. Lack of reforms of labour and product markets limit both the benefits to show up in faster poverty reduction. More challenges ahead is to introduce reforms in anti-poverty programmes.

Reforming Anti-Poverty Programmes

Anti-poverty programmes are mainly run by the Central government. They amount to 6-7 per cent of total Central government expenditure and 1 per cent of GDP. Even accounting for inflation they have been growing at 10 per cent annually since 1992-93. Rural works, self-employment and food subsidy are the three elements of the programme. All three food subsidy programmes make up about 55 per cent of total Anti-Poverty Programme (APP). By far the largest food subsidy programme is the Public Distribution System (PDS) was targeted towards the poor in 1997 and renamed as Targeted Public Distribution System (TPDS). Recent research in U.P. has shown impressive improvements in its performance in targeting the poor. Poor found to be four times as likely as the non-poor to purchase subsidised foodgrains through TPDS.[11]

Self-employment programmes make up only about 5 per cent of total APP spending but have received a lot of publicity largely on account of the poor performance of Integrated Rural Development Programme (IRDP). The programme was scraped in 1998, along with five other small self-employment programmes and have been renamed as the Swarnajayanti Gram

Swarojgar Yojana (SGSY). This programme has been better designed. It has replaced subsidised lending to individuals under IRDP by subsidising lending to self-help group as it has advantage of peer-group pressure lending to higher repayment rates and it has demonstrated its potential in other developing countries.

Rural works programmes account for nearly one-third of APP spending. It has two schemes, the Employment Assurance Scheme (EAS) and the Jawahar Rojgar Yojana (JRY) now renames as Jawahar Gram Samriddhi Yojana (JGSY). The EAS is an employment generating scheme and continuing with better targeting for poorer States and districts. The JRY which was also an employment generating scheme has been redesigned as JGSY is different in two aspects from its earlier form. First, it is being exclusively implemented by Gram Panchayats or village local government, and second, its main function now is infrastructural development, employment generation scheme relegated to a secondary one. Since JRY failed both to develop durable assets due to poor targeting and abuse and to provide employment to the poor. This change became inevitable for more and better infrastructure. The need has arisen to reform the EAS as the burden of providing a rural safety notes falls mainly on it.

There is no denying the fact that the better rationalisation and targeting in the APP are big step forward, there is still a long way to go on the ground. The findings of a study which showed good targeting of the TPDS also found that only 40 per cent of the grain allocated to the State actually reached to the intended beneficiaries, 20 per cent was not simply lifted from central storage facilities, and the remaining 40 per cent was uncounted for.[12] To reduce leakages and abuse, and to promote appropriate guidelines and transparency, access to information, and accountability the Central government could make participation by the States, and local government, in APPs conditional on good governance.

Challenges Ahead

Sustaining growth for poverty alleviation requires higher and more efficient investments and intensified reforms in all sectors of the economy. To enhance the country's development goals for creating an environment for people to live a long, healthy and creative life, challenges ahead are to raise both production possibilities and demand for goods and services, which alone will be able to reduce poverty. Increasing returns to investments will be, however, conditional on second generation of reforms which will reduce persistently high fiscal deficits, overcome its tremendous infrastructure bottlenecks, improve the efficiency of its financial sectors, and liberalise parts of the economy that still remain highly regulated.

Reforming agriculture at faster rate for enhancing its growth rate is an imperative need of the hour for poverty eradication programmes to succeed.

In the beginning of the last decade, agricultural growth rate was both accelerating and spreading more evenly across States and agricultural performance was remarkable is no longer sufficient to boost agricultural growth in the near future. The lack of fundamental agricultural reforms is acting as bottleneck on the sector's growth potential. In want of crucial reforms the beneficial impact of exchange rate devaluation and the reduction of manufacturing sector protection that virtually eliminated anti-agricultural bias and improved terms of trade are no longer sustainable for agricultural growth. Increase in productivity due to technological change is being gradually eroded. As a result, long-term prospects for agricultural growth and scope of higher agricultural wages and returns are shrinking and so will rural off-farm employment opportunities. Besides, real rural wages fall or stagnated in seven major States of Andhra Pradesh, Bihar, Gujarat, Karnataka, Rajasthan, U.P. and West Bengal and grew at much slower rate in four States of Haryana, Maharashtra, Orissa, and Punjab.

These are worrying signals of challenges ahead and indicate an urgent need for policy reforms to turn agricultural performance around. Public resources spent on non-targeted subsidies for power, water and fertiliser use are not only the main source of large fiscal imbalance; they also contribute to costly resources misallocation and inefficiencies that often extend well beyond agricultural sector. In their place growth and development enhancing public expenditure programmes can reverse declining productivity growth. Strong empirical evidences elsewhere suggest that public investment in rural infrastructure, rural services and human capital encourage private investment and production in agriculture. That private and public, domestic and foreign technology development and dissemination, rural infrastructure, irrigation and human capital are the major determinants of productivity growth in agriculture.[13]

Given the challenges that the nation has previously met and mastered and the foundation that has been laid during the last decade for faster growth it is altogether possible, poverty can be reduced in the days ahead more rapidly and more effectively than in the past provided the challenge of poverty reduction must remain at the forefront of official concern and become the subject of the same imaginative, through, change minded actions, as its experiments in stabilisation and structural change. Public policy and investments at the same time, need to concentrate on improving the provision of infrastructure and social services to underprivileged. Financing for such programmes can come from cutting large share of resources being absorbed by input subsidies to agriculture and from eliminating ongoing inefficient and ineffective anti-poverty programmes. The areas most in need of reform and added investment are efforts meant to raise the human capital of the poor. The need of the hour is a second generation reforms which alone will spur the stagnated poverty reduction.

NOTES AND REFERENCES

1. Government of India, *First Five-Year Plan* (People's Edition), 1953, p. 1.
2. Between 1951 and 1997, The NSSO has undertaken 38 national household survey.
3. Government of India, "Approach Paper to Ninth Five-Year Plan (1997-2002)", January, 1997, p. 1.
4. Government of India, "Ninth Five-Year Plan (Draft)", Vol. 1, p. 3.
5. *Ibid*.
6. The reason is not clear.
7. World Bank (1999), Indonesia: Country Assistance Strategy Processed.
8. World Bank (1999), India: Reducing Poverty in India: Options for More Effective Public Services, p. 4.

9. World Bank (1998), *op. cit.*, pp. 6-7.
10. World Bank (1997), Primary Education in India.
11. World Bank (1999), Kriesel, S. and S. Zaidi, "Thar Targeted Public Distribution System in U.P.".
12. *Ibid*.
13. World Bank (1996), *India: Five Years of Stabilisation and Reform and the Challenges Ahead*, New York, Oxford University Press.

6

Creating an Enabling Environment for the Poor

In India, as elsewhere, social outcomes both embody poverty and represent a way out of poverty. Malnutrition, poor health, lack of learning opportunities, and limited choices are defining characteristics of poverty. Good education, health and nutrition and low fertility help reduce poverty by increasing opportunities to generate income. And an improved standard of living leads to gains in health and education, freeing people from the trap of ignorance and exposure to disease. There has been a positive correlation between health and education. Education enables people to use information better for making healthy behavioural choices. Healthy people are more likely to attend school or go to work and can learn and work more effectively. Unfortunately, costs of illness keep people in poverty. Poor quality education limits opportunities to escape poverty.

Improvement in the social sectors is both a vital yardstick of and a key element in the reduction of poverty. There are constitutional and often repeated governmental commitments for ensuring basic education and health services. Substantial improvements have been made during the last 50 years. Nevertheless, social indicators continue to suggest surprisingly low level of literacy and school enrolment and surprisingly high levels of infant mortality, maternal mortality, and malnutrition in comparison to China, Indonesia and other low income developing countries. Within the countries inter and intra-State disparities are large. The poor, rural women, disabled and people belonging to Scheduled Castes and Scheduled Tribes stand out as the most vulnerable sections of society. The indicators in Table 5.1 suggest substantial problems in the States where poverty is high. It would be difficult task to reduce poverty in the days ahead without major improvement in spending on and in delivery of health and education services in these States.

The delivery of public services in health and education is fraught with problems related to limited accountability for performance, low management and worker incentives, inadequate materials and equipment for effective health care and education, demand for free social services and subsidy for both merit and non-merit services. Because of these problems, private, delivery of health and education is expanding rapidly to which the poor have little access.

In this chapter these issues are discussed in detail. The health and education sectors are examined in terms of their outcomes. Besides, the infrastructure, human and financial resources and institutional issues common to health and education have been analysed in detail. The constitutional obligations and policy pronouncements be effective for the rich and the poor alike only when if spending is made more effectively on elementary education and basic health systems, with better targeting for the poor, and with more State funding to address the unfinished agenda. By realigning the role of the State towards primary health and education and making efforts to widen the role of private sector in higher education and curative health services and effective and efficient use, the challenges in the days to come will be effectively met.

Creating an Enabling Environment: 50 years of Performance

Greater coverage and more effective elementary education in grades 1-8 would be the education sector's most significant contribution for alleviating poverty. Rising income and expanding education have allowed everywhere to improve their health. Conducting economic policies for sustaining growth across the world has resulted in increasing the health of the people.[1] Improvement in health always pay in terms of increases in incomes, productivity and substantial improvements in living standards.

Primary education is crucial for health, people who have had more schooling seek and utilise health information more effectively than those with little education or no education. Education of girls and women is more beneficial to household health as they are the overall incharge of household activities.

Average educational and health outcomes have improved but they have a long way to go for the poor. The country still lag behind comparator countries. The literacy rate has risen from 52 per cent in 1991 to 64 per cent in 1997, a rise from 64 per cent to 73 per cent for males and from 39 per cent to 50 per cent for females. But the number of illiterates[2] which has actually risen from 1981 to 1991 begun to decline in 1990s.[3] Some of the poorest States for example, Bihar, Orissa and Rajasthan registered significant improvement in literacy, albeit from low bases. More significantly, in these States women literacy rose even more faster than overall literacy.

Although the increase in literacy rate was impressive in recent decades, it still has to go a long way. Many countries, including China and Indonesia have overtaken India in literacy rate. In 1950, China had problems of illiteracy that were similar to India's at that time. By the middle of the last decade, China virtually eliminated illiteracy in the younger age group.[4]

Indonesia, on the other hand, has achieved 85 per cent literacy, with a female literacy rate of 80 per cent. With current annual growth rate of 2.75 per cent the country will take sixteen years to achieve Sri Lanka's current literacy rate of 90 per cent, even then about 110 million people will still be illiterate.

Gross enrolment ratio have also improved reaching 90 per cent at primary stage, with girls enrolment reported to be 73 per cent.[5] Despite the improvement, 33 million children in the 6-11 age group are still out of school. The NSS also suggests that 7.8 per cent girls and 6.9 per cent boys in the 6-11 age group are in the work force monthly in rural areas.[6]

A major factor behind the low enrolment rates is less enrolment of children from poor households. The poverty gap in enrolment is large. The enrolment rate is 25 percentage points lower for the poorest households having per capita annual income of less than Rs.3,000 than for the richest households with annual per capita income of Rs.10,000 and above. And the drop out rate for the poorest households is about four times that of the richest ones. In fact, the major deterrent to school enrolment among the poor is its high cost.[7] The few empirical studies of learning achievement also suggest that primary level learning achievement is low among the children from poor households, and that it varies from State to State and with the background of the child. Low-income children in the North and East are particularly worse.[8]

Health outcomes are no different from education. Between 1970-93, life expectancy at birth increased from 50 to 61 years, infant mortality decreased from 137 to 74 per 1,000 live births. On the demographic front, the conditions prevailing at the time of launching of family planning programme in 1951, have radically changed. By 1992, fertility had declined to 3.6 with per women compared to 6 four decade ago. There has also been commendable successes relating to specific diseases in recent years. Leprosy cases has declined and polio has nearly been eliminated. Yet, in India despite such significant improvements, it remain below, East Asian 'Mercle' economics even after their recent crisis and below many African countries.

Malnutrition is a major problem for the poor. The country has a high percentage of malnutrition. It has the highest levels of malnutrition in the world in certain sections of population. Working children and women most suffer from malnutrition. During the last two decades there has been modest decline in the levels of severe and moderate malnutrition in the children. 53 per cent of children below 4 years continue to be moderately or severely malnourished. Only Bangladesh has the highest level. Micronutrient deficiency is also widespread. A nation-wide survey found that 87 per cent of the pregnant women are anaemic because of iron deficiency. The economic losses due to malnutrition are estimated to cost at least $10 billion annually.[9]

The poor suffer largely from these problems. In 1992-93, compared to the richest 20 per cent of people, the poorest quintile had about 2.5 times the infant mortality and under 5 mortality rates, double the fertility rate, and nearly 75 per cent higher rates of child malnutrition.[10]

In 1997, infant mortality rates were as high as 96 per 1,000 live births in Orissa, 94 in Madhya Pradesh, and 85 in Uttar Pradesh and Rajasthan per 1,000 live births.[11] On the other hand, Kerala had remarkably low rate of 12 deaths per 1,000 live births followed by 47 in Maharashtra, 51 in Punjab, and

53 in Tamil Nadu. The gaps between States are widening as better off States shown the most rapid declines in infant mortality during the last decade. There are also large differences between districts within States. Poor people are the most suffer everywhere.

Health care services must reach the women. There has been gender basis in its approach. The gender disparity—the ratio of females to males is below one whereas in the rest of the world outside Asia the percentage of females is higher to males. This gender disparity suggests a need to make health care, nutrition, and social rights of women more equitable. The largest gender disparity are found in the States of Haryana and Punjab, despite their being two of the most prosperous States. Only Kerala has a female to male ratio above one.

Health and education outcomes are closely related to each other. Research has demonstrated that the early years of a child's life are critical for cognitive and psychological development.[12] Child development is determined not only by the status of the infant, but it also affected by the total, synergistic impact of health and nutritional factors and the quality of social interactions and stimulation received from the environment. Integrated child development programmes in operation since 1978, its limited impact on child development an enabling environment is a cause of concern for the country.

Characteristics of the Services

Major challenges are being faced by the social services caused by growing population, industrialisation, and globalisation of the economy. These place a premium on information technology, stretching the capacity of educational system to deliver relevant and effective services. The task remain to be fulfilled as yet are: getting 33 million children from poor households into primary schools, increasing the retention rate to enable more children to finish primary grades and improving the average quality of the schooling received. In the health, an epidemiological transition is taking place in the country. There continues to be high rates of communicable diseases, malnutrition, and maternal and parental illness, representing a large unfinished agenda that predominantly affect the poor.

Elementary education in the country has seen a few positive developments in the recent past. Important among them are bringing elementary education to the fore as a priority issue and introducing a series of externally funded and centrally sponsored projects including the District Primary Education Development Programme (DPEP). The DPEP has been designed to enhance government efforts to provide basic education to all children in the age group of 6-11 years with a focus on girls, marginalised communities, children with disabilities and working children. The programme supports interventions for expanding access to primary school or its equivalent for all children, increasing retention and improving student learning achievement levels and enhancing the capacity of institutions at all levels for effective management of primary education.

The Programme covers at present 149 districts of 14 major States. It has seen a great deal of innovation and experimentation aimed at qualitative improvement of the services offered by the system. Though successful innovations and experimentation have been well documented, the large educational system continues to raise challenges and concerns related to quality and management.

The problems of health care services is being addressed by the Ministry of Health and Family Welfare more strategically. The accountability of public sector health services has improved a lot because of decentralisation efforts in some of the States and some of the States are focusing on improving services to under-served tribal areas. The role of the private sector has also been recognised by the government.

Institutional Arrangements: The Emerging Issues

Education and health are the joint responsibilities of the Central and the State governments. Finances are provided by both levels of government and delivery of services is largely a State responsibility. In education dramatic change in the system is taking place with the introduction of Panchayati Raj Institutions at lower levels of government within the framework of the 73rd and 74th Constitutional Amendments. Devolution of responsibilities is expected to improve education by generating more community support, more school level responsibility for effective instruction and a decentralised resource support. But such a devolution may lead to increased uncertainty as States would decide which responsibility to be transferred to lower levels of government. The process of devolution of responsibilities need to be accompanied by planning and training to ensure effective financing and management at lower levels of government. Decentralisation is not stifled by new regulation need utmost care. Enabling environment to be created needs effective support of media to make aware people with their rights and responsibilities. This is a formidable challenge.

In health care, the existing financial and administrative set-up is complex. It hinders effective financing and accountability for decentralised management of health facilities and deterring effective coordination across the health, population and nutrition sectors. The financial transfer mechanism and many institutional structures are ineffective in providing essential inputs, correcting inequities between States, strengthening decentralised management and monitoring programme performance. There is an imperative need for greater field-level coordination and integration of nutrition services with health and family welfare.

Inadequate Infrastructure

Public education and health require enormous infrastructure and staff. These services are thinly spread over the country. Day-to-day management of these services over the length and breadth of the country, training personal and upgrading the system is a difficult task. Facilities for these services are often in disrepair, poorly equipped and their bias toward salaries and new construction rather than maintenance. Absenteeism of staff in these services is very common in the rural areas. These services at lower and middle levels are underutilised because of these reasons. Consequently the quality of health and education suffers. At the same time, tertiary hospitals are overcrowded and the number of classrooms and teachers have not kept pace with the growth of school-age population. Presently, there are only 49 students per teacher in India which is much higher than Indonesia which had 21 students per teacher in 1993 spread fairly evenly across the provinces.[13] It is estimated that 1 million more classrooms and 0.6 million more teachers would be needed to enrol the entire 6-10 age group.

Poor Financing

Public sector financing education and health are low by international standards. Central and State governments combined expenditure in 1996-97 was equal to 4.9 per cent of GDP for all levels of education and 13.4 per cent of total government revenue expenditures. It was somewhat below the average of 17.5 per cent for all low income countries.[14]

While the Central government's share is a relatively small part of total educational expenditure of the country. It was 14.6 per cent in 1996-97. Most of these expenditures are needed to create and sustain new programmes. This gives the Central government a greater role in influencing the evolution of the system than meeting the needs of its expenditure. State expenditures on education as a share of State domestic product (GSDP) are somewhat below the peak levels and vary considerably across the States. In 1995-96 States education spending ranged between 3.7 per cent of GSDP in the major States and 16-29 per cent as share of total State expenditure.

In the distribution of general government spending among educational levels elementary education which benefits most the poor and help creating an enabling environment, receives per student a much smaller level of funding and subsidy compared to secondary and higher education.[15] The fund going to elementary education is constant at 1.5-1.6 per cent of GSDP. The composition of the expenditure on various needs in elementary education is highly unbalanced. Recent studies indicate that salaries account for about 97 per cent of educational development expenditures in lower primary schooling and 96 per cent in upper primary schooling while 0.2 per cent of GSDP is spent on the other components.

The coverage of elementary education needs to be broaden among the poor and improve its quality and enhancement of its funding for achieving the goal of universalisation. No doubt, in the past few years, the government—both the Centre and States—have indicated their intent to increase public spending on education to 6 per cent of GDP during the Ninth Five-Year

Plan. Keeping in view the importance of elementary education in reducing poverty and the fiscal problems being faced, there need be to reduce implicit and explicit subsidies on higher education. Since many of the States are facing financial crunch, the Central government should expand its role in elementary education to create an enabling environment for the poor to develop their skill, improve capabilities and get opportunities for work.

Like education in health also public spending is very low. An estimated 1.2 per cent of GDP is being spent on health. Such low spending places the country amongst the lowest quintile of countries. In terms of maternal and child care, the spending per capita is one-third less than the recommended amount by an international agency.[16] Public spending on preventive and promotive primary health care services has not kept with the growth of demand for services, particularly for people below the poverty line.

The States cover nearly three-fourths of public spending for the health sector. They mainly finance primary health care facilities, hospitals, and aspects of disease control programmes. Central spending emphasises family welfare, nutrition, and disease control programmes. Moreover, capital spending is shared equally by the Centre and the States. Like education in health too, resource allocation has been skewed in favour of tertiary care services and much of the spending is absorbed by salary costs.

Despite their deteriorating fiscal situation, some States including Andhra Pradesh, Karnataka and West Bengal have manage the resources for health and have initiated systematic changes. In general, public sectors health spending is significantly lower in poor States, where health outcomes are also poorer. The mechanisms used by the centre to fund health programmes to reduce inter and intra-State disparities have not succeeded in overcoming inequities. Contrary in some cases even have exacerbated them.

Private Sector and Social Outcomes

Total private spending in education is estimated at about one-third of total educational expenditure. Private spending in elementary education generally takes in any of three forms. These are (i) schools which cater to lower income groups, charge very low fees, and provide students with little more than basic literacy, such schools are generally not recognised or aided by local governments; (ii) schools that cater to middle income groups, charge higher fees and are aided; and (iii) schools that charge very high fees and cater to an exclusive minority of the upper middle class and above. Private spending on elementary education is expanding rapidly because of the inability of the public system to deliver and parental ability to pay. In U.P. 36 per cent of school-going children were enrolled in private schools. In other northern States, the proportion ranges from 5 per cent to 11 per cent. A recent study indicated that even poor families and disadvantaged communities arc making great sacrifices to send children to private schools, with one-fifth coming from families involved in casual labour and one-half from Scheduled Caste or backward caste groups. Parents consider private schooling as being more accountable and demonstrating higher level of teaching activity, especially in terms of teaching in English.

Although private spending is being encouraged by both the Central and the State governments to supplement their own efforts, the private schools are unlikely to improve the education of the poor directly. In fact, they are, widening the gap between the rich and the poor.

Public spending on health being low, overall spending is high because of private spending. Private spending in health is four times public spending. It is about 80 per cent of health spending and being one of the highest in the world.[17] As a result, overall expenditure on health is about 6 per cent of GDP among the highest in the region. However, there are large inter-State variations in private financing and provision the lowest proportion of private hospital care are in rural Orissa and highest in rural Bihar.

Despite high spending on health reflecting high private spending, health indicators are relatively poor for the poor, health indicators present a dismal picture. The private sector motivated by profit alone is unlikely to improve the health and nutritional status of the poor substantially. Private spending and delivery neglect, public goods or inequalities reducing health services. Though the private sector includes highly trained specialists. As in education, the failing of public sector health services are leading to rising demand for private services. The public sector has an important role to play for people to have a long and healthy lives.

Poor Outcomes for the Poor

The poor are often not reaping benefits from public health and education services as their costs are enormous burdens for the poor. The direct cost of education excluding opportunity cost, is nearly prohibitive for the poor households. The lowest per capita household expenditure on education in Bihar, having lowest per capita income and large number of people below poverty line was 7.3 per cent for the households having less then Rs.3,000 annual income according to a study conducted during 1994.[18] During the same period, in Kerala this percentage was 21.4. These cost are a lower fraction of higher income groups, spending. Desegregation of educational expenditure into different heads reveals that school uniforms, books, and stationary absorb a major part of the total expenditure. Nowadays the emerging business of private coaching and transport also substantially contribute to the expenditure. Naturally in these circumstances, elementary education becomes a major financial burden for poor households having several children of school-going age. It has been observed that the probability of children in rural areas being in school increases by 11 per cent if they belong to the second rather than in poorest quintile, and increases with each level of household wealth.[19] So also, school attendance is lowest in the poorest quintile compared to the wealthiest quintile in all States, with the largest gaps between rich and poor found in Bihar, Punjab and Rajasthan and lowest in Kerala and North Eastern States.[20]

The mere presence of a school in a village, though increases enrolment by 4 per cent, does not guaranteed quality education. Poor parents are more likely to withdraw their children from school in situations where teachers are often absent or the quality of teaching is poor. Thus, improving the quality of education is not a requirement for children already in school but a powerful lever for increasing enrolment of the poor.

Health too absorbs a significant portion of poor households' income but often the spending on public health services do not yield much benefit. In general on an average, households spend 5-7 per cent of their income on health but the rural households below the poverty line spend 12-19 per cent of their income on health. The poor also benefit less from health services. The benefit of these services go to the richest 20 per cent. The large unqualified practitioners, most found in rural areas and urban slums, are mostly consulted by the poor. Consequently, health gaps between rich and poor is widening.

The goal of reducing poverty will remain elusive as long as poor have low utilisation of preventive and curative health services, poor hygienic conditions, low school enrolment and attendance, and poor quality schools and health service. Despite the longstanding recognition that health and education for creating an enabling environment is a public responsibility, as enshrined in the constitution and pronounced in policy statements, these problems are continuing even after 50 years of Independence.

The Alternatives that have been Tried

Official commitment, civic cooperation and demand from society are the three pillars on which the structure of the enabling environment are being created in the States. Experience of Himachal Pradesh is an example in recent years for others to emulate. It has demonstrated the key measures required for improving primary education. The measures being official commitment expressed in resource allocation, parental demand that their children be educated, and civic cooperation in supporting schools. Besides policies and strategies have been designed to suit the local needs and conducive for betterment of existing environment keeping in view the interests of disadvantaged groups.

Even if there is a political will and needed resources for the same, evidence suggests that improvements in education must emerge from the community and at the school level. Success of developmental programmes based on cooperation and not on command. Programmes beneficial to the whole society may succeed by direction from above. Their success depends mainly on community participation. Education guarantee scheme in Madhya Pradesh, Lok Jumbish and Shiksha Karmi in Rajasthan and District Primary Education programme provide on excellent examples. The decision to assign responsibility for elementary education to Panchayati Raj institutions provides a mechanism for adapting these schemes. What needed most is meticulous planning and effective execution.

In the era of globalisation and increasing compilation, when more power has also become a traded goods, success of a programme will depend on its marketing. A clearly articulated vision of schooling incorporating expectations of community about children learning and teachers with devotion will provide needed marketing strategy.

However, in a country like India where wide disparities exist in social outcomes the resources that are used for improving primary education need to be targeted at those groups that are most in need of support. The programme design need to include all the disadvantaged groups including girls of all groups. The poor States in terms of social outcomes like Andhra Pradesh, Bihar, Madhya Pradesh, Rajasthan, Uttar Pradesh and West Bengal where more than half the school-age children do not attend school need to spend more on primary education from their budgetary resources. With State initiative, central support and private sector cooperation, no doubt, an attempt for creating an enabling environment is being made.

Like education public investments in health are critical for the creation and sustainability of development and poverty alleviation. Recognising this fact Ninth Five-Year Plan has identified health as one of the six priority areas and emphasised integration of vertical health programmes; better surveillance and control of communicable and non-communicable diseases; improved health management information system; strengthened logistic management; and facilitation of Panchayati Raj institutions involvement in health. The Central Council of Health and Family Welfare too has recognised the importance of linking the preventive and promotive care with selective aspects of health care.

For creating health environment for the people in general and the poor in particular, the strategy must incorporate the following for reforming the health sectors for its wider reach.

These are: (a) using public information more strategically to empower consumers of health care and enable people to the better providers of their own health care; (b) rejuvenating the public sector to better deliver its care services; and engaging the private sector to better meet societal health goals.

The useful information for improving healthy behaviour and to better enable public accountability of health services accountable to the public is critical but underdeveloped in want of universal elementary education. A better educated empowered people needs to become a force for higher standards in both the public and private sectors. Many States have undertaken steps to help promote this. Both Central and State governments have initiated programmes to make public health and nutrition more strategic and less ad hoc, moving beyond the distribution of messages raising awareness and concentrating on changing behaviour to improve health.

For creating an enabling environment for health of the people the public sector needs to find ways to focus on better delivery. The prime function of government today is to develop a culture of performance. This would help create an enabling environment which include not only improvements in public service provision, but also in oversight of the health sector to protect the public interest. Many functions in the health sector including appropriate policy development, information dissemination, regulations, mandating are underdeveloped. The emerging problems of globalisation in the health sector could be better solved by (i) reviewing the fiscal structures and procedures in the health sector, including the role of Central, State and Panchayati Raj institutions' financing in the provision of basic inputs, (ii) developing budgeting and management tools facilities at district, State and Central levels for better planning, utilisation and monitoring of resource-use against the progress of important health options; (iii) developing fiscal tools to enable greater experimentation with resource allocation, alternative financing mechanism, and with regard to choices between provision versus financing of health care services; and (iv) finding ways to share responsibilities and coordinate activities between the Centre and States in the areas of health, family welfare and nutrition. However, there is an urgent need to focus on improving the quality of services.

In the changed economic environment the private sector can no longer be ignored, but instead needs to be engaged as an agent to meet the basic social goals of education and health. The process of private sector participation has begun in a variety of ways. What is needed in the change situation is to undertake studies for better understanding of the dynamics of private sector provision and its financing and identifying the problems which needs public-private cooperation.

The Way Ahead

A renewed commitment for social outcomes is needed if the poor are to reap the benefits of better education and health. The attempts that are being made to form a common agenda for social outcomes by strengthening public-private cooperation will smoothen the path ahead. Moreover, what is needed most is to enhance our understanding of the factors that would improve delivery of basic health and education, particularly to the poor. While more spending is needed, the framework for public-private partnership and incentives would need to change in order to make spending more effective. The steps that are needed to improve the reach of the poor are:

- (i) Spending more effectively on elementary education and basic health system, with better targeting the poor, and with more public funding to address the unfinished agenda;
- (ii) Focusing public education and health services on meeting consumer needs;
- (iii) Realigning the role of the State to focus on primary education and health and water and sanitation, while making efforts to upgrade private education and health services and to use them effectively, and
- (iv) Meeting health needs of the children.

India's future will depend on its children where the greatest returns on its investment is still live. In view of the independent nature of health and education needs of children there is a need to strengthen linkages among each sector. More spending in the same manner is not what is needed. The system for resource allocation and political overseeing of health and education have led to technically inefficient and inequitable allocations. The thinly dispread system needs widening in all its dimensions. Creative and vigorous processes are also needed to generate greater demand for higher quality and more accountable education and heath services. This would necessitate finding ways to increase the involvement of communities in the planning, monitoring, financing and oversight of social services. Carefully planned decentralisation of education and health resources and accountability can facilitate the process.

Where the government has assumed its primary role in creating an enabling environment as provider of social outcomes, it may become more effective in increasing the quality and quantity of services and in making them available to the poor. Equity in social outcomes will alone provide an environment for the people to live a long healthy and creative lives.

NOTES AND REFERENCES

1. Sinha, R.K., 1999, *Reforming World Economies: Lessons for India* (Chapter 2), Anamika Publishers and Distributors (P) Ltd., New Delhi.
2. Aged 7 years and above.
3. World Bank (2000), "India: Reducing Poverty, Accelerating Development", p. 22.
4. Dreze, G.P. and J. Leh (1995) "Literacy in India and China", *Economic and Political Weekly*, November 11, 1995, pp. 2868-78.
5. National Council of Education for Research and Training (NCERT), 1998, Sixth All-India Educational Survey, National Tables, Vol. 4, New Delhi.
6. Government of India, *Sarvekshana*, Vol. 21, No. 2, 73rd Issue, NSSO, Deptt. of Statistics, Ministry of Planning, 1997.
7. Parents need to spend about Rs.318 per month per child, besides opportunity cost to the family that rises with the child's age. Sec. PROBE Team (1999) Public Report on Basic Education in India, Oxford University Press, New Delhi.
8. Filmer, D. and L. Prikhet (1998), "What Educational Production Function Really Show", Policy Research Working Paper No. 1795. World Bank, Washington D.C.
9. World Bank, "India: Washing Away: The Crisis of Malnutrition", Report No. 18667-IN, Washington D.C.
10. World Bank (1999), "Health and Poverty in Fact Sheet, India

1992-93", India Poverty Consultation Workshop Processed.
11. Government of India, NSSO, NSS 52 Round survey.
12. Young, M.E., 1996, Early Child Development: Investing in the Future, World Bank, Washington D.C.
13. It is a student per teacher for U.P. and Bihar, the largely populated and poor States in India.
14. United Nation Development Programmes (1993), *Human Development Report*, Oxford University Press, New York.
15. National Institute of Public Finance and Policy, (NIPFP) 1977, Government Subsidies in India, New Delhi.
16. $15 per person in developing world as a whole was recommended by World Development Report 1993, p. 69.
17. World Bank (1997), *op. cit.*
18. National Council of Applied Economic Research (1994), Non-Enrolment, Drop-Out and Private Expenditure on Elementary Education. A comparison across States and populations groups.
19. Lanjouw, P. and M. Ravallion (1998), "Benefit Incidence and Timing or Programme Capture", Development Research Group, World Bank.
20. Felner and Princhett, *op. cit.*

7

Reforming States for Reducing Poverty

The Centre and the States are the two players in creating environment for development and growth in the economy. But States play a key-role in devising and implementing policies to reduce poverty, promote human development, and stimulate growth. The Constitution of India has also assigned significant responsibilities in major sectors of the economy. These include agriculture, industry, infrastructure, education, health, social welfare, and tax and expenditure policy at the State level.

The economic reforms that have been launched since 1991 hold the promise of considerably improving the living standards of the poor. The economy has responded well to the reforms and the government has explicitly committed itself to accelerate the development of the human resources. By maintaining its commitment to economic liberalisation and reforming fiscal structure, improving the effectiveness and targeting of spending in education, health, and infrastructure, and anti-poverty programme, the long battle of reducing poverty will get a new impetus.

Worldwide experiences suggest that where policies have increased growth particularly in agriculture and human development poverty has fallen faster. In contrast where growth was slow, or where human development policies lacking, or ineffective or misdirected to the politically more-advantaged, poverty reduction has been relatively slow. This is equally true in the case of States in India. On an average, the higher income States grew faster than other States from 1980-81 to 1997-98, with exception of Tamil Nadu and Rajasthan. This divergent growth pattern widen the gaps in per capita income among States, despite efforts to achieve balanced growth in the country.

During a decade of reform all the high and middle income States except Rajasthan accelerated their pace of growth because of their initial leads in governance, infrastructure and human development, these States derive maximum benefit of macro policy reforms. In contrast, growth slowed in poorer States. Bihar the poorest State, experienced a decline in per capita income. Growth also slowed in agriculturally prosperous States of Haryana and Punjab, the richest States in 1991. These States failed to take advantage of new opportunities created by macro policy reforms because of weak governance, infrastructure, and human resources, and in case of Haryana and Punjab, growth was restricted by limited reforms in agriculture.

The slow growing poor States of Bihar, Orissa, Uttar Pradesh constitute nearly 40 per cent of country's population. Unless these States improve their performance, it will be increasingly difficult to reduce poverty in the country. Primarily the improvement has to come from their own efforts, given their major roles in human development, infrastructure, and governance. The poor States have received favourable fiscal transfers from the Centre and further enhanced transfers is unlikely to come in view of their poor performance and the Centre desire to reduce its large fiscal deficit. However, the Centre could support State reforms through its own reforms to improve governance, the civil service, the system of inter-governmental transfers and tax reforms. On their part, the States need considerable improvements in their governance, institutions and the regulatory environment and in their social and physical infrastructure. Consequently fiscal deficits will be reduced through cuts in inefficient spending including inequitable subsidies and supporting reforms in power, irrigation and regulatory framework in general and encouraging private factor.

With sustained political commitment, the States can improve their policy environment, put their economy on higher growth path, and narrow the disparities with rich States regardless of their economic conditions. Reforming the States economy could substantially decrease overall poverty in the country.

Differential Growth Widen Disparities

Balanced regional growth has been an important objective of

the successive Five-Year Plans and States have been helped by redistributive transfers from Centre to States.[1] Nevertheless, as evidenced from Table 7.1 that on average, the middle and high income States grew faster than the low income States during 1980-81 to 1996-97. The high income State's per capita annual growth rate of 3.9 per cent was almost twice the low income States, per capita annual growth rate of 2.1 per cent. The middle income States growth rate per capita per annum was 3.2 per cent which was nearly 50 per cent higher than low income States.

Consequently, ranking of the States in terms of per capita income changed marginally since 1981. Between 1990-91 to 1996-97, Rajasthan and Tamil Nadu achieved the highest growth rates of 4.7 per cent and 4.1 per cent per annum respectively. Rajasthan accelerated its growth rate because of heavy investment in infrastructure whereas Tamil Nadu derived the benefit of better initial conditions in human resources and heavy investment in irrigation. Their rapid growth rates moved Rajasthan up from low income group to middle income group and Tamil Nadu high income group.

During the decade of reforms growth differentials accentuated, with growth increasing in the high income States of Gujarat, Maharashtra, and West Bengal and in middle income States except Rajasthan. In contrast, growth slowed in most of the low income States, as well as in the two highest income States of Haryana and Punjab. The change in policy environment, with liberalisation of trade and investment regime, allowed the States a major role in determining their development paths and attracting investment. Gujarat, Maharashtra and many of the middle income States were able to take greater advantage of the changed conditions because of better initial conditions, good governance, adequate infrastructure and developed human resources. In want of these low income States lagged behind. With the exception of Orissa, poor States failed to improve their State level policies to offset their initial disadvantages in attracting new investment. As a result their growth slowed down and GDP per capita declined. Agriculturally predominant States of Punjab and Haryana, with limited reform in agriculture too experienced slow growth.

The widening growth differential naturally translates into a

TABLE 7.1: Real Per Capita Income of the 14 Major States

States	Per capita income						Growth rate (per cent)		
	Per capita	Rank	1990-91	Rank	1996-97	Rank	1980-81	1990-91	1996-97
High Income	2385		3269		4377	–	3.2	6.1	3.9
Punjab	3020	1	4163	1	4935	2	3.3	2.8	3.1
Maharashtra	2671	2	3826	3	5358	1	3.7	7.4	4.4
Haryana	2647	3	3864	2	4392	3	3.7	2.6	3.2
Gujarat	2200	4	3047	4	4221	4	3.3	8.6	4.2
West Bangal	1912	5	2349	6	3146	6	3.1	4.9	3.2
Middle Income	1607	–	2659	–	2676	–	3.0	4.2	3.2
Karnataka	1690	6	2295	7	2988	7	3.1	3.4	3.6
Kerala	1690	7	2106	8	2705	8	2.2	4.9	3.0
Tamil Nadu	1677	8	2514	5	3297	5	4.1	5.2	4.3
Andhra Pradesh	1543	9	1997	10	2432	10	2.6	3.8	2.9
Madhya Pradesh	1508	10	1951	11	2205	11	2.6	4.1	2.4
Low Income	1308	–	1725	–	1804	–	2.8	1.8	2.1
U.P.	1418	11	1842	12	1997	12	2.6	1.8	2.2
Orissa	1415	12	1555	13	1833	13	0.9	1.5	1.6
Rajasthan	1373	13	2170	9	2533	9	4.7	3.9	4.3
Bihar	1062	14	1374	14	1245	14	2.6	0.7	1.0
All States	1715	–	2310	–	2842	–	3.0	4.4	3.2

Source: CSO.

TABLE 7.2: State Poverty and Social Indicators and Their Standard Deviations

	Population below the poverty line[a]			Literacy[b]			Female literacy			Birth rate[c]			Infant mortality[d]		
	1978	1994	Rate of chance (%)	1981	1991	1997	1981	1991	1997	1981	1991	1996	1981	1991	1997
Maharashtra	67.8	43.5	2.7	53.5	64.9	74.0	39.6	52.3	63.0	29.8	25.2	23.2	79	59	47
Punjab*	26.9	21.6	1.4	46.4	58.5	67.0	38.4	50.4	62.0	30.2	26.3	23.5	81	56	51
Haryana	–	–	–	41.7	55.9	65.0	25.8	40.7	52.0	35.9	30.9	28.8	101	75	68
Gujarat	39.9	33.8	1.0	49.9	61.3	68.0	36.9	48.6	57.0	34.2	28.0	25.5	116	67	62
Tamil Nadu	54.9	34.9	2.8	52.6	62.3	70.0	39.4	51.3	60.0	27.9	19.5	19.2	91	58	553
West Bengal	51.8	26.0	4.2	46.3	57.7	72.0	34.4	46.6	63.0	32.0	25.7	22.8	91	65	55
Karnataka	52.9	37.6	2.1	43.9	56.0	58.0	31.7	44.3	50.0	29.1	25.5	23.0	69	73	53
Kerala	53.2	29.2	3.7	78.9	89.8	93.0	73.4	86.2	90.0	24.9	17.4	17.8	37	17	12
Rajasthan	51.6	43.5	1.1	28.4	38.6	55.0	13.4	20.4	35.0	40.1	34.0	32.3	108	90	85
Andhra Pradesh	47.0	29.4	2.9	34.1	44.1	54.0	23.3	32.7	43.0	30.8	24.3	22.7	86	71	63
Madhya Pradesh	63.9	44.1	2.3	32.2	44.2	56.0	18.0	28.9	41.0	38.5	34.9	32.4	142	104	94
Uttar Pradesh	46.7	40.2	0.9	31.4	41.6	56.0	16.3	25.3	41.0	38.4	36.2	34.0	150	98	85
Orissa	62.1	40.3	2.7	38.8	49.1	51.0	24	34.7	38.0	34.0	27.2	26.8	135	115	96
Bihar	64.8	60.4	0.4	30.3	38.5	49.0	15.8	22.9	34.0	37.2	32.0	32.1	118	73	71
Standard deviation	0.24	0.26	–	0.27	0.23	0.17	0.45	0.38	0.27	0.13	0.20	0.19	0.34	0.44	0.49

*Data for population below poverty line for Punjab include Haryana.
[a]Per cent, based on World Bank India Poverty Assessment 1997.
[b]Per cent of population of seven years and other.
[c]Per thousand population.
[d]Per thousand live births
Source: MoF, Economic Survey; Ministry of Human Resources Development, Annual Report 1997-8; World Bank staff estimates.

widening dispersion of State per capita income, an unusual result compared to other countries. Inter-State inequality has declined in U.S.A., Canada, Europe, Japan and Australia and Indonesia. However, inter-regional inequality is significantly higher in India compared to other large federal States. In 1980-81, the highest State per capita income in Punjab was 2.8 times more than the lowest in Bihar. This ratio increased to 4.3 in 1996-97. If the trend continues, the ratio may increase to 7.5 by the end of another decade.

Although the share of population below the poverty line declined and human development indicators improved in all States, progress was significantly faster in fast growing States which are higher income States.

As evidenced from Table 7.3 among the major States, Kerala and West Bengal had the fastest rate of poverty reduction, faster than several more growing States. Human resource development in Kerala made Keralists to emigrate internationally and generate remittances that raised income and reduced poverty in ways that are not captured by its GSDP. However, the large poor States cannot adopt this strategy very well, given their poor levels of human development, their weak fiscal situations that limit the availability of funding for human development, and the difficulties in emigrating the workforce elsewhere. In West Bengal land reforms and high agricultural growth over the period seems to be factor influencing growth.

Reforming States: The Need of the Hour

During pre-reforms decades the development strategy and intergovernmental transfers shaped the development policies of the States. During those period they could not depend on private capital for their development. National policies excluded it from important sectors and, where permitted, central licensing authorities, and not the enabling environment, determined the volume and composition of private investment. Consequently, a State's pace of development was determined by its ability to expand public investment in agriculture, infrastructure and manufacturing. For this, States relied largely on Central government.

States dependence on intergovernmental transfers discouraged fiscal discipline among the States. Large transfers built expectations discouraged States not to mobilise resources since ever-expanding and politically more expedient financing would be forthcoming. As a result, throughout the 1970s and 1980s, the States expanded investments in physical infrastructure and provision of social services without establishing mechanisms for cost recovery and for maintaining these assets in the long-run. Prices charged for power, water, irrigation and other services declined.

By the second half of 1980s it became evident that the States were experiencing considerable fiscal difficulties. They had created a large infrastructure and expanded social services without establishing adequate tax base or price mechanisms to recover their cost, finance their maintenance or ensure their needed expansion. They had expanded public employment to the point that in most States wages and pensions absorb between 4-5 per cent of State GDP, and 9-10 per cent of GDP was not infrequent in the States of Rajasthan, Andhra Pradesh, Orissa, Uttar Pradesh and Bihar. They had contracted debt without establishing the financial base for its servicing. They punched welfare programmes that could not be sustained in the long-run. As a result fiscal stress became evident. This resulted in decline of spending on capital, education, health, and operations and maintenance while spending on interest payments begun to rise as seen in Table 7.3.

Most of the emerging infrastructural bottlenecks that are being faced today is due to insufficient and declining resources for operations and maintenance. These trends were accelerated by the stabilisation and reform programmes launched a decade ago. Central transfers ceased to grow and eventually started to decline. Financial liberalisation resulted in rise in interest rate resulting in large interest payment. Gradually but persistently, most States found themselves unable to play their role in providing key infrastructure services and developing human resources.

Reforms for Reducing Poverty

Accelerated, labour intensive development strategy is needed to reduce poverty among the States where poverty concentration is the largest. Speeding up country's development will

TABLE 7.3: State Government of Finances 1980-1997 (India 1997. P. 25 T.22)

(per cent of GDP)

	1980-81	1985-86	1989-90	1990-91	1991-92	1992-93	1993-94	1994-95	1995-96 R.E.	1996-97 B.E.
Revenue receipts	12.0	13.0	12.9	12.6	13.2	12.9	13.0	12.8	12.4	11.7
Tax revenue	7.7	8.4	8.6	8.4	8.6	8.6	8.5	8.4	8.5	8.4
State own taxes	4.9	5.6	5.7	5.6	5.8	5.7	5.7	5.8	5.8	5.7
State share in central taxes	2.8	2.9	2.9	2.7	2.8	2.9	2.7	2.6	2.7	2.8
Non-tax revenue	4.4	4.6	4.3	4.2	4.6	4.4	4.5	4.4	3.9	3.2
Of which grants from centre	2.0	2.6	2.4	2.5	2.5	2.5	2.6	2.1	1.9	1.8
Revenue expenditure [A+B+C]	11.0	12.6	13.2	13.4	14.0	13.6	13.5	13.5	13.5	12.8
A. Development (1+2)	7.7	8.8	8.9	9.1	9.5	9.0	8.8	8.2	8.4	7.8
1. Social services	4.4	5.1	5.3	5.2	5.0	4.9	4.8	4.7	5.0	4.7
2. Economic services	3.4	3.7	3.7	3.9	4.4	4.1	3.9	3.5	3.4	3.1
B. Non-Developmental	3.1	3.6	4.1	4.1	4.3	4.5	4.6	5.1	5.0	4.9
Of which interest payments	1.1	1.4	1.7	1.7	1.8	2.0	2.0	2.1	2.1	2.2
To centre	0.7	0.7	1.0	1.0	1.1	1.1	1.2	1.2	1.2	1.2
To others	0.4	0.6	0.7	0.8	0.7	0.9	0.9	1.0	0.9	1.0
C. Transfer to local bodies	0.2	0.2	0.1	0.1	0.2	0.2	0.1	0.1	0.1	0.2
Net current balance	1.1	0.4	–0.3	–0.8	–0.8	–0.7	–0.5	–0.6	–1.1	–1.2

Capital expenditure [A+B+C]	3.8	3.1	2.6	2.5	2.1	2.2	2.1	2.3	2.3	2.1
A. Development (1+2)	2.3	2.0	1.7	1.7	1.6	1.5	1.5	1.8	1.5	1.4
1. Social services	0.3	0.3	0.3	0.2	0.3	0.2	0.2	0.2	0.3	0.3
2. Economic services	2.0	1.8	1.4	1.4	1.3	1.2	1.3	1.5	1.3	1.1
B. Non-Developmental	0.1	0.0	0.1	0.0	0.0	0.0	0.0	0.0	0.1	0.1
C. Loans and advances (net)	1.5	1.0	0.8	0.8	0.5	0.7	0.5	0.4	0.7	0.6
Gross fiscal deficit	2.8	2.7	2.9	3.3	2.9	3.0	2.6	2.9	3.4	3.3
Finance by instrument										
Market loans	0.2	0.5	0.6	0.5	0.5	0.5	0.5	0.4	0.5	0.4
Loans from centre (Net)	0.9	2.7	1.7	1.8	1.5	1.2	1.2	1.4	1.3	1.3
Small savings & provident funds	0.3	0.4	0.5	0.6	0.5	0.5	0.5	0.5	0.4	0.4
Other	1.4	-1.0	0.1	0.5	0.4	0.7	0.3	0.5	1.2	1.2
Memo items										
Primary Deficit	1.7	1.3	1.2	1.6	1.2	1.0	0.6	0.8	1.3	1.1
Total Debt Outstanding	17.6	20.5	20.6	20.6	20.5	20.2	19.8	19.3	19.4	19.3
Of which: Owed to Centre	12.1	13.4	13.6	13.4	13.1	12.8	12.3	11.6	11.7	11.5

Note: BE = Budget estimates; RE = Revised estimates.
Source: Ministry of Finance, Union Budget; Reserve Bank of India, RBI bulletins of state finances.

depend heavily on better performance in the poor States. However, their improved performance will depend largely on their own efforts, given their major roles in human development, intra-State infrastructure and the inter-State regulatory framework. States during the previous years have received large loans and transfers from the Centre but this trend will continue in the future is difficult to predict in view of the need for fiscal prudence and the way these funds have been misutilised by the States. However, the Centre will provide the needed support for creating an enabling environment for economic growth.

In such a situation accelerated development in the States will depend on greater public and private investment to speed up their growth, greater efficiency in the use of investment, and improved human development. These are not feasible in the absence of reforms at the State level. Reforms will be needed to improve governance and institutions in general and strengthening transparency, increasing accountability in service delivery, reducing opportunity for discretion and improving expenditure management and administration in particular. Besides, physical and social infrastructure needs improvement which will entail supporting reforms in State finances, power and irrigation, and the regulatory framework. Such reforms and development spending will create an investment-friendly environment to attract private capital that is badly needed for growth.[2]

States' Fiscal Performance in the Era of Reforms

The States marginally adjusted to the fiscal crisis of 1991, almost exclusively by cutting their capital and human development in the early years of the 1990s as shown in Table 7.4.

This pattern of fiscal adjustment raises questions about the sustainability of long-run development and poverty reduction. The States made only limited attempts to raise revenues by increasing users charges and bringing untaxed income into tax net. In fact, they engaged in competitive populism and 'tax wars' to lure investment.[3] The States also allowed their non-development spending rising as percentage of GSDP caused by increase in interest burden and wage bills.

TABLE 7.4: Main Fiscal Trends in All States

(per cent of GDP)

	1990-91	1991-92	1992-93	1993-94	1994-95	1995-96	1996-97	1997-98 (RE)
Total revenue	11.5	12.1	11.9	12.0	11.8	11.2	10.8	11.3
Own revenue								
Tax	5.2	5.4	5.2	5.3	5.4	5.2	5.0	5.4
Non-tax	1.6	1.9	1.7	1.8	2.1	1.9	1.7	1.6
Central transfers	4.6	4.8	5.0	5.0	4.3	4.1	4.1	4.3
Shared taxes	2.5	2.5	2.7	2.6	2.4	2.4	2.5	2.6
Grants	2.2	2.3	2.3	2.4	1.9	1.7	1.6	1.8
Total expenditure	14.7	15.0	14.7	14.4	14.4	13.8	13.5	14.6
Revenue expenditure	12.4	13.0	12.6	12.5	12.4	11.9	12.0	12.6
Interest payments	1.5	1.6	1.7	1.8	1.9	1.8	1.8	2.0
Education	2.7	2.6	2.5	2.5	2.4	2.4	2.3	2.5
Health and Family Welfare	0.8	0.8	0.7	0.8	0.7	0.7	0.7	0.7
Capital expenditure (net)	2.3	2.0	2.1	1.9	2.0	1.9	1.5	2.0
Revenue deficit	0.9	0.9	0.7	0.4	0.6	0.7	1.1	1.3
Fiscal deficit	3.2	2.9	2.7	2.3	2.6	2.6	2.7	3.3
Debt stock	18.7	18.6	18.4	18.3	17.8	17.4	17.2	18.2

Note: New GDPmp series is used (revised base 1993-94) and for years prior to 1993-94 rebasing is done assuming a linking factor. Fiscal year ending on 31 March.

Source: RBI States Supplement 1998, CSO.

By the year 1998-99, the deterioration in fiscal performance pushed the deficit back to the 1990-91 level. The States' fiscal deficit worsened to 4.2 per cent well above the 3.2 per cent in 1990-91 and there is no significant change thereafter. Moreover, the composition of State public spending has worsened further, with increase in revenue spending and decline in development spending.

The reform of State finances has become inevitable as fiscal deficit has reached unsustainable levels. The gross fiscal deficit to GDP ratio of State governments touched an all time high of 4.2 per cent in 1998-99. The fiscal performance of individual States varied widely during the 1990s, with the most marked deterioration in some of the poor States. In Uttar Pradesh, fiscal deficit rose from 4.5 per cent of GDSP in 1993-94 to 8.4 per cent in 1997-98, in Bihar from 4.0 per cent to 6.2 per cent, and in Orissa from 5.7 per cent to 6.3 per cent. However, fiscal deterioration was not limited to poor States only, it also deteriorated in Kerala and Rajasthan.

Rising deficit placed the States in heavy debt. In Uttar Pradesh the debt-SGDP ratio rose from 26 per cent to 31 per cent, in Bihar from 35 per cent to 42 per cent, and in Orissa from 41 per cent to 43 per cent. Financing these large deficits has meant increased borrowings and guarantees. The States are limited in their domestic borrowing by the Central government and 60 per cent of their debt is to the Central government. The Central government passes the fund that it borrows on their behalf at its average cost, which has been rising with financial liberalisation. The States are constitutionally prohibited from borrowing abroad and have reasonably tight limits on overdrafts by the Reserve Bank of India.

The States have been able to ease the budget constraints through, in some cases temporarily access to the RBI, build-up or arrears to suppliers and campaigns to stimulate relatively high cost, small savings that are largely funnelled back to the State that mobilise them.

State government guarantee have also been used to circumvent the hard budget constraints. During first half of 1990s State Public Enterprises were given separate borrowing allocations for each year as part of State-specific overall ceilings for the statutory liquid ratio (SLR) and market borrowing. With the removal of these limits, State guarantees given to the SPEs have become a convenient means for States to circumvent the ceiling imposed on borrowing by the Central government. This issue has assumed growing importance in recent years because of rapid increase in these liabilities. The volume of State guarantees increased from Rs.403 billion in March 1992 to Rs.796 billion in September 1997, representing a compound rate of growth of 12 per cent a year.[4]

These States with large deficits are on unsustainable development paths given the high real cost of borrowing and the crowding out of development spending by interest costs, salaries and subsidies. This has caused revenue deficit to rise. The political environment and weak reforms by the States suggest that it will be an enormous challenge to restore their fiscal health and strengthen the development impact of their spending.

The Needed Reforms

State-level reforms that would correct the deteriorating fiscal situations and enhance their development capabilities would include efforts towards improving the tax system, reforming public enterprises, reprioritising spending and improving cost recovery. These measures would reduce fiscal deficit to a sustainable level, encourage private investment, and ensure public spending effective impact on poverty alleviation and development.

In fact, fiscal crisis has spurred some of the poor and most indebted State governments to embark on a path of comprehensive reforms, similar to economic restructuring programme launched by Andhra Pradesh. The reform efforts are aimed at restructuring State level expenditure and improving governance so as to maximise the outcomes achieved by public spending and private investment in the State; and enhancing the revenue base through tax policy and administrative reforms and cost recovery from publicly provided non-merit goods and services.

A number of reform initiatives that are the responsibility of the Centre would help improve the general policy environment for all States. They include agricultural reform.[5] Elimination of small-scale industries reservation, removal of barriers to inter-State trade, providing leadership and incentives to politically sensitive measures.[6] Unless supportive measures are taken in the poorer States, the second generation of macro reforms would continue benefiting mainly the high and middle income States.

Economic reforms of the last decade has radically changed framework within which States' development policies are implemented. States now can attract private capital in sectors such as power, irrigation, ports, road and all areas of manufacturing. And it is their ability to attract private capital which will determine a State's growth performance. Development spending in the change environment needs to be more narrowly focused on the State's areas of comparative advantage, where it complements rather than supplement private sector.

However, attracting private capital requires States to provide an enabling and investor-friendly environment. Such an environment needs good quality and abundant infrastructure, an educated labour force, a business-friendly public administration, and moderate levels of taxation. These require significant reforms as stated earlier. In particular, it requires

(i) Policy, pricing, institutional and regulatory reforms to translate private sector interest to invest in infrastructure into commercially viable ventures and improvements in the States' capacity to manage commercially enforceable contacts.
(ii) An environment conducive to efficient public investment in areas wherein public sector will remain important.
(iii) Public spending restructuring to eliminate wasteful expenditure and make room for priority programmes in public infrastructure, health and education.
(iv) Tax reforms to provide stable sources of revenue at low efficiency cost.

In many States, policy, pricing and institutional reforms of key sectors would bring the needed fiscal restructuring. Power and irrigation sector reforms would generate large fiscal gains in virtually all States. In States of Maharashtra, Karnataka and Gujarat, such reforms done would be sufficient to restore fiscal sustainability. In States of Andhra Pradesh, Rajasthan, Tamil Nadu, West Bengal, and Haryana putting the States' finances on a sustainable path would require more comprehensive reforms of public expenditure. And poor and highly indebted States of Orissa, Bihar and Uttar Pradesh sectoral reforms and public spending restructuring need to be complemented by debt refinancing.

Reforming power and irrigation would be the centre piece of the reforms strategy at the State. Explicit and implicit subsidies are highest in these sectors. These are not only costly, but also indicate inefficiencies. Without reforms and improved cost recovery, it would be difficult to encourage private provision of power or better use of irrigation. Therefore, improvement in cost recovery in those sectors on a sustained basis and sector restructuring are essential to restore sustained growth and sustainable State finances.

The sector in almost all the States faces the crisis of severe power shortages and heavy financial losses are State Electricity Boards (SEB), arising mainly from theft and provision of almost free power to farmers. The subsidies are a major factor for the deteriorating State finances. Depoliticalisation of tariffs and management of the utilities, and restoration of credit worthiness in these sectors are essential to attract private sector funds. The needed reform would typically involve separation of generation, transmission and distribution of the SEB, setting up new independent companies operated commercially under Companies Act to carry out these activities. Besides, setting up an autonomous Electricity Regulatory Authority is also needed to regulate tariffs.

Several States have started to implement these reforms. Many States including Orissa, Gujarat, U.P., Rajasthan and Haryana have adopted a new power policy that endorses:

(i) creation of an independent regulatory agency,
(ii) tariffs reflecting costs,
(iii) competition among independent power producers,
(iv) divesture of shares in the power generating public companies, and
(v) restructuring and privatisation of distribution functions of the SEB.

This approach was laid out in a Common Minimum National Action Plan for Power (CMNAP), issued by the Ministry of Power in December 1996[7] and steps have been taken to implement it. However, Punjab, Bihar and Kerala have already back-tracked from the CMNAP's objectives by offering free electricity to farmers.

Effective expansion of irrigation is key to ensuring sustained agricultural growth and reducing rural poverty. The States normally allocates substantial public funds for the development of canal irrigation network. However, the benefit of these investments are not fully realised because those funds are thinly spread over too many projects, leading to substantial time and cost overrun. In addition, operations and maintenance (O&M) activities are adversely affect the efficiency of the system. The main reforms in the irrigation sector would include adequate budgetary provision for O&M expenditure, substantial improvement in cost recovery, greater participatory involvement of farmers,[8] transfer of revenue collection and O&M responsibility to WUAs and improvement in institutional and legal systems. Encouraging private sector participation in infrastructure through creation of a supportive legal and policy environment and improvement in delivery of social services by strengthening institutions and training staff and also priority areas for reform. It is important for State governments to create an enabling environment that attracts fresh investments and improve private sector participation in their development process. Without these sectoral reforms both fiscal sustainability and accelerated growth would be very difficult to achieve.

Investment for rehabilitation and modernisation, combined with value-based pricing and institutional change would provide the basis for efficient water use, cost recovery and improved service delivery. Tamil Nadu, Andhra Pradesh, and Orissa were the first to initiate reforms that would lead to improved cost recovery, quality of service delivery to farmers and systems turnover to water users. Karnataka in its 1995 agricultural policy resolution, proposed radically to transform institutional incentives in the irrigation sector, but has been slow in implementing reforms.

Other States showing an increasing commitment to reform include Haryana, Gujarat, Rajasthan, U.P. and M.P. A worrisome development is the policy back-tracking in Punjab and Maharashtra. These development make it politically more difficult to improve cost recovery in these sectors in other States.

Fiscal Transfers: Need Redesigning

Indian system of fiscal transfers has a number of positive features. It provides a transparent rule-based framework which makes transfers predictable. By subjecting State borrowings to Central government approval and precluding access to international finance, it has imposed a relatively hard budget constraint and spared the country from the moral hazards and macro economic crisis witnessed in federated States of Latin America—many of which were triggered by State governments excessive borrowings with the implicit Central government guarantee. And, over the years, successive Finance Commissions have attempted to reduce regional inequalities by recommending higher per capita levels of financial support to poorest States. However, the system also provides perverse incentives to States to increase the size of their development plans and current expenditure without adequate regard to expenditure priority, debt sustainability and resource mobilisation.

The weaknesses of the system of transfers have been acknowledged by States through their memorandum submitted to the various Finance Commissions and recently by the Ninth Five-Year Plan.[9] Under the theme of cooperative federation the Ninth Plan proposes to move with the States to a more flexible approach to the transfer, design and coordination of development strategies. Specifically it proposes that the National Development Council suggest changes in grant-loan formula while also considering the question of inter-State distribution of assistance. The plan also proposes to remove the bias in favour of the large plans by delinking the size of the plan from the level of Central assistance to the States.

Fiscal decentralisation is the need of the hour and it should match the ongoing devolution of powers with fiscal resources to enable local governments to spend on public goods and services they are responsible for. The Central government intends to increase its dialogue with States on fiscal reform and plan implementation and devote more attention to periodic surveillance and implementation of agreed commitments by States. The new initiative which involves policy conditionability by the Centre for their resource transfers to States, as evidenced from the terms and conditions of Eleventh Finance Commission and its recommendations is a welcome development and a good step towards nationalisation and modernising the intergovernmental transfers.

However, much scope exists for additional reforms. Further liberalisation of banks and financial markets would provide opportunity for the creation of a competitive market for States government securities. But meaningful reform is unlikely to occur unless financial institutions are free to reject to debt issue of financially weak States and the Central government rejects the implicit full guarantee against default and establishes a transparent set of rules for highly indebted States.

Other policy options which could be considered are

(a) Consolidating centrally sponsored schemes to reduce administrative costs and partly converting them into block funds;
(b) Clarifying the constitutional assignments of indirect taxes and the exchange of rental of taxing powers to permit the implementation of a dual VAT; and
(c) Designing the new financial institutions or market structures to intermediate the borrowings of State governments so that they can finance their increasing infrastructure needs without creating moral hazard problems for the Centre.

The most difficult challenge lie ahead is the restructuring of spending policy. Besides improved cost recovery the unproductive expenditures need to be reduced. Size of the government needs to be curtailed for reducing wage bills which has substantially increased with the implementations of Fifth Pay Commission Report. Welfare programmes need to be consolidated into a limited number of well-defined and targeted schemes. States also need to resist implementing centrally sponsored schemes which they consider an additional source of revenue, without examining their relevance to State priorities. In order to limit the interest burden, a more careful selection of projects based on their rate of returns needs to be established. SPEs need to be subjected to a hard budget constraint by discontinuing the practice of converting debt in equity. Privatisation of enterprises engaged in activities that could be provided commercially by private sector efficiently and effectively will provide sustainability to State finances.

Such measures would enable the States to mobilise resources for critical spending on rural infrastructure and human resources thus arresting declines. States subsidies account for 7 per cent of SGDP, almost twice total spending on health and education. Spending on health and education are not only a small fraction of State GDP but this has been declining since 1991. There is a scope to enhance efficiency of service delivery, cost-effectiveness and allocations of expenditure. But spending needs to increase as well. However, in the fiscally strained circumstances, it may be more realistic in the short-run to aim for a phased re-orientation, of outlays so that higher proportion go to the primary and secondary sectors that benefit the poor most. Besides, restructuring spending, there is scope for improvement in revenue side also. Reforms need to focus on improving the efficiency of taxation and ensuring tax harmonisation across States.

Such a reform with "human face" will help achieve the goal of poverty alleviation promised fifty years ago by founding fathers of the Constitution.

NOTES AND REFERENCES

1. Sinha, R.K., *Regional Imbalances and Fiscal Equations in India*, South Asian Publications, Delhi.
2. Govinda Rao, M.R.T., Shand, and K.P. Kalirajan (1999), "Convergence of Income Across Indian States: A Divergent View", *Economic and Political Weekly*, March 27, pp. 269-78.
3. Kurian, N.J. (1999), "State Government Finance: A Survey of Recent Trends", *EPW*, 8-14 May, pp. 115-25.
4. Total outstanding guarantees accounted for almost 9-10 per cent of SGDP in September 1997 and varied from 4 per cent in U.P. to 14 per cent in Punjab.
5. Such as reduction in distortionary subsidies, improved pattern of public spending, deregulation of agricultural sector and rural finance and empowerment of poor through participation.

6. Such as elimination of industrial incentives by State government, harmonisation of State taxes, improvement of cost recovery and the regulatory framework.
7. The objectives and content of the programme have been inspired by the pioneering reform in Orissa several years ago when in State started implementing comprehensive power sector reform.
8. Through constitution of Water Users' Association (WUAs) in its management.
9. Government of India, Ninth Five-Year Plan, 1997-2002, Planning Commission, Chapter on Cooperative Federation.

8

Good Governance for Reducing Poverty

The business of a government is good governance. Good governance is not a luxury but a necessity for development and poverty reduction. Good governance is a major contributor to development, while people living in ineffective or venal States suffer from a lack of economic and social development and bread poverty. Key institutional and capacity elements of good governance are a comprehensive legal framework defended by an impartial and competent judicial system, accountable, open, and transparent executive decision-making coupled with a capable flexible, and efficient bureaucracy and strong civil society participation. Good governance ensures effective property rights and contract enforcement without excessively restrictive and arbitrary structures, and the delivery of an appropriate mix and quality of the public services, with the inclusion of the poor and women, and without corruption.

Corporate governance, on the other hand, refers to the procedures and rules, explicit and implicit, that provide the incentive framework for companies to attack financial and human capital, perform efficiently and avoid corruption. The crisis in East Asian Countries have highlighted the importance of corporate and financial governance systems supportive of market processes and competition and the huge costs stemming from weakness of such institutions. Good corporate governance is necessary for efficient allocation and use of reforms within a more transparent framework and help promote private investment.

Weak or arbitrary property rights and contract enforcement are important factors in underdevelopment. They deter saving and investment both domestic and foreign. The poor are hurt not only by lower investment and growth of labour demand, but because they cannot count on speedy, low cost enforcement of their contracts and protection of their property. Excessive limits on contracts performance and poor enforcement are likely to end up hurting the poor. Corruption weakens contract enforcement and property rights and it is anti-poor. Opportunities for corruption increase with the number and complexity of rules, licenses, taxes, and subsidies.

The formulation of good policies and efficient service delivery are critical for development and poverty alleviation. An efficient and honest bureaucracy is a key factor for encouraging investment for development. Efficiency in delivery of public services is particularly important for the poor, such as primary education and health to improve their lot and mitigate the risk they have. Non-transparent budgeting and spending, widespread subsidies, and corruption are likely to lower the efficiency and equity of public spending. Lack of accountability and poorly directed incentives and disincentives in the government and civil service mean that such problems are likely to remain unsolved and responses to crisis will be weak. Good corporate governance is essential for economic growth. With investors in emerging markets becoming more cautious, good corporate governance will be critical for attracting foreign investment.

The State is an agent of development and market is an agent of growth. Good governance enables the market to function effectively to facilitate growth. Good governance in the corporate sector increases the efficiency of the market to spur growth. Good governance makes the State capable and good corporate governance enhances the efficiency and productivity of the market. Only a capable State and efficient market would create an environment for sustainability in growth and development to help achieve the goal of eradicating poverty. Such an environment in the economy would provide for all people to develop and grow in an environment where people would lead a long, healthy and creative lives.

Measurement of Good Governance

While governance is certainty a critical element for development and growth, its evaluation is complex and methods to do so are still in their infancy. However, effort has been made to evaluate procedural quality in governance by the countries based on various survey materials and results by key service outcomes. Since much of the data have been derived from opinion surveys, often based on perception and reflecting different cultural and legal milieus, they are subjective in nature and cannot be taken as definitive. Yet in terms of such indicators, India fares about average among developing countries on governance though it ranks well below developed countries.[1] This is due to its strong domestic traditions, free press, independent judiciary, and high civil service which have been strengths of its governance.

However, the international comparison of its governance is not in conformity with findings of domestic business. According to the survey conducted in 1999,[2] over 50 per cent of domestic business firms see the government as efficient. Of the different areas covered in the survey, telephone services, which have been now liberalised substantially, have the highest efficiency rating next to the armed forces. Health, legislative services, and road have been worse with 49 per cent to 68 per cent of respondents rating services as inefficient. The survey also highlighted business concern about the uncertainly surrounding legislation and regulatory framework, despite its predictability having increased during recent past. Though judicial system and legal machinery ranks about 50th percentile in the international cross-section, and is generally trusted by business, 64 per cent of the domestic firms found the court system expensive and 88 per cent found it slow. Besides inflation, that surveyed domestic firms consider labour regulation, corruption, poor infrastructure and policy instability as the most serious obstacles to their operation and growth.

'Outcomes' of governance tend to be worse than the evaluations of its governance processes, especially in public service delivery, which suggest implementation problems as discussed in an earlier chapter. No doubt, over the last twenty-five years, the country has done relatively well in achieving growth, achieving higher rate than all but East Asian countries. However, this growth has not been sufficient to substantially reduce the number of people living below the poverty line and also the measured reduction has slowed recently. Fruits of growth have not been shared by all. When fruits of growth distributed equally in the society based on the needs of people, it leads to development.

Moreover, spreading the fruits of growth will depend on the quality of governance and the institutional capability of the State. But growth will much depend on the functioning of the market, its efficiency and the business environment created by the governance of the State and the corporate sectors. The elements of good governance of the State will provide much needed economic and social fundamentals for development and the elements of good corporate governance will spur growth.

Neither the governance of the State nor of the corporate sector has been able to create an enabling environment for an efficient and competitive market to spur growth by using a part of the fruits of growth for spreading in the society for its development.

The greatest weakness of State governance is its legal framework that are inhibiting the economic change. This slow down the industrial and corporate restructuring and contribute to corporate misgovernance which are onerous for small-scale industries[3] and leave room for subjective interpretation and could hence lead to harassment and corruption. Some of these deficiencies have been recognised in the legislative agenda that have been put forward to the successive Parliament. These deficiencies have also been discussed in detail in the Report on Legal Adjustment and Reform for Globalising Indian Economy (LARGE).[4]

No doubt, India's judiciary is respected for its integrity and sagacity, but the issue of justice delayed is justice denied is a major problem. This point is borne out in the survey on Indian firm's perception of the efficiency of court system. With 28 million cases pending and mounting arrears, it can take up to twenty years before a decision is obtained and enforced, putting judgement beyond the reach of the poor.

Causes for such delays are many. These include under supply of judicial resources, under equipped courts, socially under priced services; cumbersome court procedures, perverse incentives to prolong litigation, and a vast body of non-transparent laws.[5] Many of them archaic are serving no purpose.

Factors contributing to delay and denial of justice and adverse incentive structures of the system have become the important issues which need solution. Factors contributing to delay and denial of justice are many. Noteworthy among them are inadequate number of judges in the High Courts and Supreme Court and the large number of vacant posts, and even worse situation prevailing in the lower courts. Adverse incentive structures often limit accountability and enforcement of sanctions against non-performing judges.

The outcome of slow judicial proceeding cause inefficiency in business environment. A study examining 1849 companies that were in the process of liquidation in the High Courts shows that in 59 per cent of these cases, the procedures took more than five years and in 32 per cent of the cases, more than 20 years. Because of inordinate delay the value got stripped by promoters and their middlemen, leaving little for unpaid workers or secured creditors. This reflects the insincerity to the cost of time and the distinction between sale proceeds and their distributions. The liquidation process is full of arcane legalities which among other things, include the preparation of audited accounts that go back several decades. A weak legal and judicial mechanism for debt recovery has been a traditional source for high non-performing assets.

To reform the system, a multi-pronged strategy is needed to ease supply bottlenecks, decrease incentives for frivolous or prolonged cases by changes in fee structures and limit admission.[6] Besides, internal government incentives to penalise officials for filing meritless cases or appeals and speeding up of the government programme to simplify laws, repealing redundant law and replacing outdated laws with new ones would help.

Corruption is another major problem weakening the rule of law, particularly affecting the social and economic environment and is a rising concern for both the Central and the State governments. Transparency, International's 1998 survey of international business perceptions ranked India worse than China and other Asian countries, and somewhat worse than other large countries. In the survey of domestic businessmen, 83 per cent reported paying bribes in transactions ranging from customs, taxes, and licenses, to infrastructure connections and government contracts.[7] These results suggest that an important cause of unsatisfactory development outcomes and business dissatisfaction with government services, may be corruption.

Reducing corruption is not an easy task when it has become a part of the system. However, it be minimised and gradually eliminated by:

(i) reducing opportunities for corruption by deregulation and privatisation, placing greater reliance on competition to ensure low prices and good quality;
(ii) improving incentives for good performance and disincentives for corrupt practices in government, and
(iii) improving administrative procedures to reduce the opportunity for corruption by increasing accountability, transparency, and the role of people voice.

Successful public administration reform for good governance would much depend on the quality of civil service and its accountability. Indian Civil Service initial capacity is among the highest anywhere, because of its meritocratic recruitment, a high level of competition in civil service examination and a mix of technically and non-technically educated intranets. Technical capability and occupational demand reasonably matched with the system of administration. Yet it has failed in its outcomes. As the principal 'face' of the government to the people and responsible for policy planning and implementation of its programmes, it must shoulder some of the responsibility for dissatisfaction with government performance in providing a business environment for growth and enhancing its capability for development.

However, the problem is not the lack of its initial capability but institutional deficiencies. Non-transparency, limited accountability, low salaries, and inadequate performance appraisal weaken the civil service administration, as do the standard problems of political interference in specific situations and government's widespread and intricate interventions that delay actions, create unwarranted power and provide opportunities for corruption. Numerous commissions have drawn the attention of the government in their reports towards these problems but most of these have been ignored.

However, some of the recommendations of the Fifth Pay

Commission would substantially improve the civil service toward good governance. The relevant recommendations are:

(i) A multi-pronged approach to employment reduction in Central government targeting a 30 per cent reduction over a 10-year period.
(ii) Restructuring and right sizing Central government services by decentralising to States, local governments, converting certain departments into corporations and entrusting certain services to NGOs.
(iii) Stopping arbitrary and frequent transfers of bureaucrats by fixing a minimum tenures.
(iv) Restructuring performance appraisal to make the current Annual Confidential Report (ACR) system more effective and open, coupled with a five-yearly high level review of senior bureaucrats (Group A), and
(v) Increased transparency by enacting a right information set.

In addition, a closer link between performance and promotions or pay increases, improved procedures to ensure individual accountability for lapses, and improved enforcement are needed for good governance. More broadly, a simplification and liberalisation of excessive restrictions, along with privatisation would reduce red tape and the scope for corruption and smoothen the path of good governance. Such steps are equally needed at lower levels of governance.

Sound Budgetary System

India's ranking of its budgetary system and efficiency in international comparisons is fairly high. However, in terms of the more general category of management of public finances, it ranks much lower in terms of its fiscal deficit, high level of implicit and explicit subsidies having negative efficiency effects and tax system with limited base.

A sound budgetary system conducive to overall fiscal discipline is one which has the following characteristics:

(a) a comprehensive annual budget with few off budget expenditures and sources of revenue;

(b) limited earmarking;
(c) expenditure planning in a medium-term framework based on consistent macroeconomic forecasts to allow forward planning;
(d) a hard budget constraints on expenditure dictated by revenue availability;
(e) a framework to reconcile actual outlays with the budget and impose sanctions for overspending and under spending; and
(f) transparent budgetary system.

Not all of these characteristics are met by the Indian fiscal system. More importantly, future revenue and expenditure implications, even for long-term capital projects are not reported or taken into account in the budget. Instead of revenue availability dictating expenditure ceilings, revenue and expenditure budgets are separate exercises, with additional resource mobilisation (ARM) measures decided on if projected sources fail to meet expenditure projections. Besides, the States are only engaged in short-term cash management with no medium term perspective or framework, unlike the Central Government, the States continue to depend on the CAG of India, both to prepare their account as well as to audit them. Furthermore, instead of sanctions, additional, post-budget expenditures are incorporated in supplementary budget affecting fiscal deficit adversely. Instead of transparency published budgetary accounts never permit annual aggregate expenditures to be determined.

Given the overall budget, the next stage in budgetary system is allocation of resources in accordance with strategic priorities. To achieve this, the important stakeholders should be consulted during budget planning, allocation should reflect strategic priorities and implementing ministries or agencies should also be consulted during budget planning. Allocation should reflect strategic priorities and implementing ministries or agencies should have the capability and freedom to manage their allocations effectively. Besides, there should be the existence of a system of reporting service delivery outcomes and institutional arrangements for facilitating transparency.

In India, there is ex-anti rather than ex-post control of expenditure by line agencies through the institution of financial advisors in each department who report both to their own department and the Ministry of Finance. The performance budgeting system for reporting of outputs and outcomes is divorced from financial reporting.

Given departmental allocations, operational efficiency and effectiveness crucially requires accountability. Accountability requires fixing individual responsibility for delivery of defined service outputs, personnel policies linked to performance to be measured by actual outputs in relation to prescribed service delivery standards and present targets. Accountability also requires independent internal and external financial and performance auditing with mechanisms for effective corrective or disciplinary action based on audit findings and 'customer' satisfaction surveys. On the other hand, transparency requires publication of programme performance reports and mechanisms to elicit client feedback on the quality of services provided. Apart from internal and external auditing, the institutional framework for service delivery meets none of these standards in its governance. Consequently, fiscal discipline is severely lacking, with inefficient allocation of budgetary resources to competing needs, lack of incentives for efficient service delivery, and limited transparency and accountability.

This has led to continued existence of implicit and explicit subsidies and heads of expenditure many of which are not transparently identified in thus budget and leakages and misuse of budgetary resources facilitated by poor budgetary control and lack of accountability and corruption. This has also resulted in non-transparent budgets, with budget estimates understating actual expenditures, which is rising in recent years. In the budgetary system borrowing requirements and the fiscal deficit is being grossly underestimated in the budgets. Inefficient and non-transparent fiscal system has resulted in arbitrary across—the board budget cuts and making unrealistic budgets unrelated to the cost of service of delivery targets. Wasteful expenditures and misappropriation of funds have become a normal feature of the fiscal system.

To have the good governance in the fiscal system what is needed most is increasing the effectiveness of the audit mechanism and establishment of an Expenditure Commission as existing institutions such as CAG and Public Accounts Committee

(PAC) too have been unable to curb mismanagement of expenditure. Broad based, efficiently administered taxes are also an essential part of a sound fiscal system. Tax reform in 1990s has mainly focused on tax structure reforms and within this largely on rate reforms. Though some progress has been made, mostly in curbing power to issue exemption notifications in recent years.

In spite of the fact that institutional reform broaden the tax base, improved the Centre-State tax powers and tax sharing and the structure and administration of States, taxes, progress in implementing administrative reform and institutional restructuring as recommended by Tax Reforms Committee is very slow. Reforming the fiscal system for good governance will fasten the process of poverty alleviation by enhancing State capability and efficiency in market.

Effective Decentralisation

Of late decentralisation is becoming a standard remedy for improving public service delivery, especially to the poor. With service providers closer to the recipients it is agreed that recipient's voice will be better heard and services adopted to the local conditions, thereby improving delivery. In fact, inherent in this argument is the issues of providing non-public goods through the market, that by the private sector and the possibility of even providing public services privately which are non-merit services. Another issue is the extent to which 'voice' as well as efficiency of delivery or use is reduced by delinking service provision from taxes, instead imposing user charges. However, the success of decentralisation depends on the enhancement of capacity at lower levels of government and a strong institutional framework not subject capture by local elite.

A promising beginning has been made following the 73rd and 74th Amendment of the Constitution. However, decentralisation is far from complete and cracks are already beginning to surface in the evolving system of fiscal and functional decentralisation. The overall situation is one of incomplete institutional development and inadequate capacity building. The efforts of the government to enhance resource base of decentralised governments needs to be accompanied by effective steps to improve the management capacity of local government.

However, without a strong resource base, the local governments will not be able to play effective role in reducing poverty. Presently local governments own revenue receipts constitute a very small proportion of total government resources. Their own revenues meet only a part of their revenue expenditure. In the case of panchayats, for which the database is fragmentary, it is estimated that own revenues cover not more than 5-10 per cent of the expenditure, making them almost wholly dependent on State government. So also, the administration or local taxes is unsatisfactory and reflected in poor collect to demand ratios, their inability to periodically adjust the property valuation tax rates and user charges to inflation, as also the high cost of administration and enforcement. By and large, these governments do not have the autonomy to select tax rates, these being either laid down by the States or approved by them. And except for municipal corporations, they do not have borrowing powers. All these adversely affect their governance and quality and quantity of services provided.

The existing accounting procedures and audit arrangements of the Panchayati Raj institutions are highly inadequate. Paucity of trained and inadequate staff is stumbling block in governance, poor resource base of the State also influence their governing capacity as they work in the overall framework within the State.

Situation at the bottom ladder of administration would be improved by: a review of the legislation; re-examining the shape for enhancing financial powers of municipal corporations, local governments and PR institutions and making available technical assistance to provide sound local government system and spread of information network for speedy transformation of information among all level of governance.

In the absence of elements of good governance there neither be growth nor its spread across the society for creating an environment for people to live a long, healthy and creative life and reducing poverty will only remain a dream.

NOTES AND REFERENCES

1. World Bank, 2000, *op. cit.*, Appendix 4.1 pp. 145-7.
2. A survey of 210 firms carried out by the Confederation of Indian

Industry and the World Bank as a part of its World Business Environment survey.

3. Small-scale industries do not have the capacity to deal with excessive regulatory and disclosure requirements.
4. LARGE was initiated in 1993 under the Ministry of Finance with involvement of the National Law School of India, Bangalore to examine economics and commercial legislation in India in order to make it more market-friendly.
5. Over 3,000 central statues and ten times of States statutes exist.
6. Such a strategy has been spelt out by the National Task Force on Judicial Reforms in its Report in 1996.
7. 91 per cent of the respondents said that the payments were less than 10 per cent value, but 2 per cent said they paid more than 25 per cent.

9

Infrastructure for Growth and Development

Infrastructure services including power, transport, telecommunications, provision of water and sanitation and safe disposal of wastes—are central to the activities of households and economic production. This reality becomes painfully evident when natural disasters or civil disturbances destroy or disable power stations, road and bridges, telephone lines, canals, and water mains. Major infrastructures failures quickly and radically reduce communities' quality of life and productivity. Conversely, improving infrastructure enhances welfare and fasters economic growth.

Providing infrastructure services to business, households and public at large is one of the major challenges of development and growth in an economy. No doubt, the availabilities of infrastructure has increased significantly in many of the developing countries over past decades. However, in many developing countries the full benefits of past investments are not being realised, resulting in a serious waste of resources and lost economic opportunities. This outcome is frequently caused by inadequate incentives embodied in the institutional arrangements for providing infrastructure services. While the special technical and economic characteristics of infrastructure give government an essential role in its provision, dominant and passive intervention by governments has in many cases failed to promote efficient or responsive delivery of services.

Sixty-two per cent of respondents to a study conducted by Confederation of Indian Industry (CII) in 1999 rated India's infrastructure as hindrance, with roads rated the worst. However, the overall rating of infrastructure, especially telephone availability and roads seems to be improving since 1996.

International investors rank India's infrastructure very low.[1]

What is Infrastructure

Economic infrastructure includes services from public utilities, public works and other transport sectors. Public utility services include power, telecommunication, piped water supply, sanitation and sewerage, solid waste collection and disposal and piped gas. Public works include roads and major dams and canal works for irrigation and drainage. Other transport sectors include urban and inter-urban railways, urban transport, ports and waterways and airports.

Infrastructure is an urban term for many activities referred to as 'social overhead capital' by Paul Rosentein Raden, Ranger Nurkse, and Albert Hirscheman. However, neither term is precisely defined, but both encompasses activates that share technical features[2] and economic features.[3]

Infrastructure can deliver major benefits in economic growth, poverty alleviation and environment sustainability but only when it provides services that respond to effective demand and does so efficiently. Service is the goal and measure of development in infrastructure. Major investment has been made in infrastructure stock but in many developing countries these assets are not generating the quantity or the quality of service demanded. The costs of this waste in terms of foregone economic growth and lost opportunities for poverty reduction and environmental improvement are high and unacceptable.

As defined earlier, infrastructure covers a complex of distinct sectors that, by any measure, represent a large share of an economy as seen in Table 9.1, taken together, the services

TABLE 9.1: Value Added of Infrastructure Services by Country Group

Sector	Low income countries	Middle income countries	High income countries
Transport storage and communication	5.34	6.78	9.46
Gas, Electricity and Water	1.29	2.24	1.87

Source: World Development Report, 1994.

associated with the use of infrastructure account for nearly 7 to 11 per cent of GDP with transport being the largest sector. Transport alone commonly absorbs 5 to 8 per cent of total paid employment.

Developmental Impact

Infrastructure, if not the engine, then it is the "Wheels" of economic activity. In developed economics telecommunications, electricity and water are used in the production process of nearly every sector, and transport is an input for every commodity. Users demand infrastructure services not only for direct consumption, but also for rising their productivity. Some cross-national studies of economic growth and infrastructure also show that infrastructure variables are positively and significantly correlated with growth in developing countries. However, in both the developed and developing countries whether infrastructure development causes growth or growth cause infrastructure is not fully established. Moreover, there may be other factors driving both GDP and infrastructure that are not fully accounted for. Neither studies of developed countries nor of developing countries satisfactorily explain the mechanism through which infrastructure may affect growth.

But sectoral studies on rural infrastructure's effect on local economy have revealed more about the nature of the apparent benefits. A study covering eighty-five districts in thirteen States in India found that lower transport costs increased farmers' access to markets and led to considerable agricultural expansion and that modern irrigation methods brought higher yields. At the same time, improved communications lowered banks costs of doing business, banks expanded lending to farmers and farmers used the funds to buy agricultural inputs resulting in increased agricultural yields. According to a village level household survey classified as "most developed" in terms of access to transport infrastructure were significantly better off than the "less developed" villages in terms of agricultural production, income and labour demand and health. From these facts one thing is evident that there exists a strong association between the availability of rural economic infrastructure and GDP. However, in low income developing countries what is most urgently needed is basic economic infrastructure such as water and irrigation and to lesser extent transport. As economy moves upwards, composition of demand for economic infrastructure give a significant change. Experiences suggest that total infrastructure stocks increase by 1 per cent with each 1 per cent increase in per capita GDP, household access to safe water increases by 0.3 per cent, paved roads increases by 0.8 per cent, power by 1.5 per cent and telecommunications by 1.7 per cent.

These relationships suggest that infrastructure has a high potential pay-off in terms of economic growth, yet they do not provide a basis for prescribing appropriate levels or sectoral allocations for infrastructure investment. Moreover, investment in infrastructure alone does not guarantee growth, it must be backed by efficient and timely use.

For developing countries to derive full benefits of globalisation, adequate and efficient infrastructure development is the first logical step. The availability of infrastructure services valued by users is critical for the modernisation and diversification of production. So also the growth of informatics is central to efficient operations in manufacturing services, the financial sector and government. The nature of infrastructure is central to its ability to respire to changes in demand and prices or to take advantages of other resources. However, infrastructure investment is not sufficient on its own to generate sustained increases in economic growth. The demand for infrastructure services is itself sensitive to economic growth which is notoriously difficult to predict. Moreover, the economic impact of infrastructure investment varies not only by sector but also by its design, location, and timeliness. The effectiveness of infrastructure investment depends on characteristics such as quality, quantity and reliability. Matching supply to what is demanded is essential.

Infrastructure is important for ensuring that growth is consistent with poverty reduction. Access to at least minimal infrastructure services is one of the essential characteristic for defining welfare. Largely poor has been identified as those who are unable to consume a basic quantity of clean water and who are subject to unsanitary surrounding beyond their immediate settlement. Consequently, they have more health problem and fewer employment opportunities.

Different infrastructure sectors have different effects one improving the quality of life and reducing poverty. Access to clean drinking water and sanitation has the most obvious and direct consumption benefits in reducing mortality and morbidity. It also increases the productive capacity of the poor and can affect men and women differently.

On the other hand, access to transport and irrigation can contribute to higher, and stable income, enabling poor to manage risks. The availability of these infrastructure expand the opportunities for non-farm employment in rural areas. The benefits of transport and communications include the access they provide to other goods and services, especially in cities. Where the poor are concentrated on the periphery of urban areas, as in many developing countries, the costs and availability of public transport become key factors in their ability to obtain employment. Access to secure and reliable public transport has been identified in household surveys in Equador as influential in determining the ability of low income girls and women to participate in evening training classes. Moreover, the construction and maintenance of some infrastructure can contribute to poverty reduction by providing direct employment.

Yet, when times are hard, capital spending on infrastructure is the first item to go and operations and maintenance are often close behind. Despite the long-term economic costs of slashing infrastructure spending governments find it less politically costly than reducing public employment or wages. Studies of fiscal adjustment and expenditure reduction find that capital expenditure are cut more than current expenditure, with infrastructure capital spending often taking the highest reduction. Moreover, within current expenditure, non-wage expenditures are cut by more than the wage bill. A World Bank review of countries adjustment experience also confirms this.[4]

Public Sector Role in Infrastructure

Production and consumption characteristics of infrastructure and its large and varied political impacts on development distinguish it from most of the goods and services.

Historically, societal needs for water supply, irrigation and flood control and transport led to the construction of engineered physical works. But modern infrastructure sectors are the result of a technology driven "infrastructure revolution" that has changed the way in which age-old demands for water, lighting, communications and waste disposal are met. The most economic characteristic of modern infrastructure is the supply of services through a networked delivery system designed to serve a multiple uses. The delivery system in most cases dedicated, that is it carries only one good. The investment in the delivery systems are mostly irrecoverable because they cannot be converted to other uses or moved elsewhere. Once paid these costs are said to be "sunk". Because the delivery system is networked, coordination of service flows along the system is critical to its efficiency. However, the scope of competitive supply of infrastructure varies greatly across sectors, within sectors and between technologies.

Demand for infrastructure derives from the activities of both individual and industries, and any interruption or restriction of supply would be seen as threat to society. Ensuring a flow of services of at least minimum quantity and quality is often considered by the government to be of strategic importance. However, because of infrastructure investments are often "lumpy" it is difficult for planners to match the availability of supply with demand at all times. Beyond consuming an "essential minimum" of certain essential infrastructure services, users have very diverse demand. And providers being monopolist, users have no choice but to pay the cost of inefficiency of providers.

However, many of the infrastructure services are almost private goods. Private goods are those that can be defined as those that are both "rival"[5] and "excludable"[6]. In contrast, public goods are neither rival in consumption nor excludable. Markets work best in providing pure private goods or services. Most of the services that the infrastructure sectors produce are excludable in a specific sense. Infrastructure services not only differ from other goods but they also differ among themselves. The characteristics of various infrastructure activities have important implications for how services should be provided. To the extent that specific infrastructure activities entail natural monopoly, they will not be provided efficiently by an unfettered market. The network component can, however, be separated (unbundled) from the more competitive activities of the sector with regulation to ensure fair access to the network. Infrastructure activities that create externalities or produce essential services to captive users may also warrant some regulations, but this can be narrowly focused on the market importations while permitting wide scope for competition in other components of the sector. Certain characteristics of infrastructure also create challenge in financing. Where a minimum level of consumption of a particular service can be identified as "life line" for some users, society may judge that they would not be excluded if they cannot afford to pay. Financing strategies also have to be designed to take account of the risk that arises because many infrastructure investments are large and long lived, while the revenue stream is often slow to develop. Such characteristics can justify some public financing of infrastructure from general revenues, but to supplement and not to substitute fully for revenues obtained from users and commercial sources of finance.

By its nature, infrastructure represents a strong public interest and merit the attention of governments. However, the special characteristics of infrastructure do not explain or justify the dominance of public sector in infrastructure services in developing countries. The dominance of public sector in the infrastructure has been influenced less by economic and much by political interests. No doubt, many countries made a impressive studies in infrastructure expenditure under the earlier stages of public leadership. But more recent experiences has yield serious and widespread misallocation of resources, as well as failure to respond to demand. Moreover, the blunt instruments of public ownership, financing and operation have not demonstrated any advantage in achieving poverty reduction goals or environmental sustainability. These deficiencies in performance are not happen at once—they are embedded in the prevailing system of institutional incentives for the supply of infrastructure.

The Performance

The record of performance is impressive but spotty. In low income economics, telecommunications, sanitation, and water supply registered the highest rates of increase in availability in recent decades, starting from a very low base in each sector. In middle income countries the growth in this period concentrated mainly in the power and telecommunication sectors, where capacity more than doubled during the same period. However, even in the middle income countries access to water and sanitation is still lacking for significant share of the population.

Infrastructure coverage has increased in both urban and rural areas. But the urban population are better served than rural population in access to drinking water, sanitation and power. Though the urban and rural do not have the same effective demand for infrastructure services but the gap in coverage of water and power have been significantly large. There is an economic case for providing power, irrigation and telecommunications in rural areas to help reduce poverty.

An analysis of how countries measure upon infrastructure coverage compared with others measures of performance is revealing. Although coverage tend to be correlated with GDP, efficiency and effectiveness of infrastructure provision are not. Moreover, it has been found that there is no correlation between a country's efficiency of provision in one sector and its performance in another. Finding of study indicates that efficiency and effectiveness of infrastructure provision derive not from general conditions of economic growth and development but with institutional environment which often varies across sectors in individual countries.[7] Thus, it is evident that changes in the institutional environment can lead to improved performance, even when incomes are low, because in each sector some low income countries have performed well and it has been found by a review of infrastructure that even many high income countries encounter performance issues which is still a major challenge for them.

Infrastructure in India

India relied almost completely on public sector provision until the early 1990s. Except for some auto-generation and limited private distribution, power, railways, roads and telecommunications were all public sector monopolies.[8] The trend towards private sector provision of infrastructure, especially in power, telecommunications, ports and airports gained momentum worldwide in the 1980s. This trend was participated by failure of the public sector in this area as well as technological advancement which enhanced the possibilities for competition.

Improved infrastructure would help reduce poverty and provide sustainability to growth yet its performance was at the lower level. Sixty-two per cent of the respondents to the 1999 CII survey rated infrastructure as a hindrance, with roads rated the worst of all public goods and services. However, the overall rating of infrastructure have improved during the post-reform era. But household connections to power and water are limited, telephone density is among the world's lowest and transportations services do not meet the needs of an increasingly mobile population.

The poor quality of infrastructure services reduces growth directly, hindering specialisation in continuous process industries and firms that depend on good quality water and power. Poor quality transport facilities raise transport costs and contribute to uncertain delivery schedule, causing business to hold large inventories and reducing the attractiveness of exports to foreign buyers. Safety problems in transport and health problems related to water availability still represent the major issues in the economy. Business routinely provide their own utility services to offset the poor quality of public services. The duplication of investment increases the capital intensity of growth. Moreover, the small private facilities are less efficient than could theoretically be achieved with well maintained high quality, large-scale works providing service through effective transportation and distribution networks.

Poverty reduction would benefit from increase in infrastructure as shown by the experiences of Punjab and Haryana. Improved infrastructure will be needed to allow the hinterland, such as Bihar and Orissa, to benefit from globalisation, along with other coastal areas. A major expansion in the availability of safe drinking water would greatly improve health among the poor. Finally, construction of infrastructure would increase labour demand given the labour intensity of construction. However, experience suggests that attempts to increase labour employment through public works programmes typically do not provide good quality of infrastructure without substantial capital and managerial inputs.

Infrastructure investment in the country would yield large benefits, both in terms of supporting higher growth, improving the lot of the poor and population at large and yielding high rates of return. Without such investment, growth could well slow down and become increasingly concentrated in coastal areas and States with good infrastructure.

Attracting Private Investment

As part of economic reform programme to attract foreign investment, doors of infrastructure was also opened to attract private investment. However, the progress has been slow. The early years of reform because of worsening fiscal situation public investment in infrastructure also declined from 4 per cent of GDP in 1991-92 to 3 per cent in 1997-98.

The full potential of the private sector for meeting pressing infrastructural needs largely remains untapped. With relatively few exceptions, there has been little progress in the way of privatisation of existing companies. However, in recent years steps are being taken to privatise the infrastructure services which are primarily in the nature of non-merit goods and need operation on commercial lines. Many regulatory authorities have been established in telecommunications and power sectors but these alone will not solve the problems and they alone will not transform an inefficient sector as regulation is an imperfect alternative to competition.

The Challenges

To determine the future demand for infrastructure it is necessary to consider efficiency with which existing capacity is being used and how well the services generated are responding to the users. No doubt, each sectors has special problems but operational inefficiencies, inadequate maintenance, excessive dependence on fiscal resources, lack of responsiveness to users needs, limited benefits to the poor and insufficient environmental responsibility are common problems for all.

The broadest indicator of inefficient performance by an infrastructure system is the extent of output lost in delivery. How to reduce it is a challenge which needs immediate solution.

Closely related to operating inefficiencies is lack of maintenance resulting in deterioration of roads, leakage in irrigation canals, breakdown in water pumps, overflowing sanitation system and frequent failure of telecommunications and non-availability of power when needed most.

Poor infrastructure policies and inefficient provision absorb scarce fiscal resources and damage macroeconomic stability. Inadequate tariffs and poor financial management has become a rule and not an exception. This has lead to inefficiency because of poor maintenance. Poor maintenance has resulted in poor quality and unreliable services which has alleviated the users.

Everywhere poor have little access to infrastructure, although with the aim of improving poor's access to infrastructure services, subsidies are being provided, but most of these subsidies are being captured by middle and the rich households. While failure to reach the poor has often been associated with flawed infrastructure pricing policies, too little emphasis has been placed on providing the poor with suitable options for the kind of services of most value to them. Appropriate services for the poor are often lacking as investment in infrastructure is on the assumption of "need-gap" rather than by an assessment of effective demand.

For economic growth environmental sustainability has often been ignored which affects the poor adversely. The negative externalities also affects the poor badly.

Many of these problems in infrastructure performance are mutually reinforcing creating serious economic and financial costs that make it more difficult to achieve greater coverage and more services to better meet social and environmental goals. Systematic problems point to systematic causes and solutions.

Directions for Change

Where infrastructure is operated inefficiently and delivers poor service, the solution cannot be simply to tell suppliers to do more maintenance and to consult users. The weaknesses in infrastructure provision are built into current institutional and organisational arrangements in which outputs and inputs are not closely measured, monitored or managed, and suppliers do not depend on user satisfaction for reward. A proper set of incentives would make managers accountable to users and to others who own and finance infrastructure facilities. It would also give managers autonomy in making decisions and responsibility for success or failure.

Infrastructure must be conceived as a "service industry" providing goods that meet consumers' demand such a commercial orientation contrasts sharply with the situation in most government departments and State-owned infrastructure providers which suffer from multiple and conflicting objectives and inadequate accounting for costs or financial risks and which put little emphasis on revenues collected and the quality of service delivered. Managers have little motivation in such circumstances to satisfy consumers or to achieve a reasonable returns on assets through efficient operation and adequate maintenance. Providers of infrastructure are subject to pervasive interference by political authorities which adversely affects operational decisions on investment, pricing, labour and technological choices. Time has come to view certain infrastructure services as potentially commercial because these are the services for which it is easier to recover the cost of services.

Competition promotes efficiency and provides users with options that in turn, make infrastructure providers more accountable. The government often take advantage of the potential for competition, even in activities where a natural monopoly does not exist. While open competition for users in the market is still not feasible in many infrastructure areas there are alternative ways of obtaining the benefit of computation.

However, in many infrastructure activities, market signals cannot be relied on to provide information about demand or to gauge performance. When users are locked into a delivery network, they cannot express their preferençes or dissatisfaction through choice. In such circumstances, other means of making service providers accountable to users are needed.

Lost Opportunities

Many of the notions discussed above are not new, and invariably they have been accepted in principle but not yet been put successfully into practice. However, technological change, more pragmatic attitudes, and a greater sensitivity to infrastructure's implication to poverty and environmental sustainability have created a new climate for reform. Innovative techniques for drawing on private financing for investment have created new challenge to traditional ways of providing infrastructure. Countries of the Third World are now taking advantage of all the emerging opportunities. India too should take advantage of such emerging opportunities.

Technological changes are creating a variety of new opportunities for changes the way infrastructure is provided all most in every sectors. Micro electronic monitoring devices and non-destructive testing techniques can facilitate the assessment of infrastructure facilities, often permitting testing by an agent and not by operator. No doubt, electronic information systems would facilitate better planning and design investments and better coordination of network operations. Emergence of more efficient, robust and flexible technologies have enable developing countries to "leaping" sectoral transition experienced earlier by high income developed countries. India should take advantage of their experiences.

A new attitude stemming from an enhanced understanding of the relative strengths and weakness of State and markets, is also creating an opportunities for reform of infrastructure provision. Worldwide liberalisation of markets and experiments with different forms of private sector participation in many sectors have provided a new body of experience to reinforce the pragmatic attitude. Theoretical and institutional advances have also revealed when regulation is necessary and how to refine its application. In the emerging global economic environment, there are fewer infrastructure activities requiring government intervention than once believed. And when required, intervention can be expected through less distorting instruments of public policy than those traditionally used.

Awareness that poor are constituencies that must be answered to, has stimulated a search for alternative ways of providing services or managing demand so as to broaden access while maintaining environmental sustainability. Spread of efficient and affective infrastructure services to poor will be most effective step in reducing poverty.

The Way Ahead

Awareness with past mistakes together with new opportunities, demands that a fresh look be taken at the respective roles of State and the private sector to play an effective role as provider of infrastructural services. The challenge is to demarcate the sectors where market can run efficiently and effectively and those where public action is needed most. Within this broad demarcation of services, there is a menu of institutional options that allow public and private groups to assume responsibility for different aspects of service provision. However, the choice among the options will vary from country to country on the basis of their economic, institutional and social characteristics. The spectrum is broad but options available are public ownership and operation through a public enterprise or government agencies, public ownership but with private responsibility for all options, private ownership and operation and community and user participation.

Running public utilities on commercial principles and using market also in infrastructural provision and taking the help of local governments and users beyond market will no doubt will introduce efficiency, increase effectiveness and bring accountability in the system to help reduce poverty by growth and its spread across society.

NOTES AND REFERENCES

1. The 1998 Global Competitiveness Report of the World Economic Forum rated India 53rd out of 53 countries surveyed.
2. Economics of Scale
3. Spill over from users to non-users.
4. The World Development Report 1994, World Bank, p. 19, Box 1.3
5. Consumption by one users reduces the supply available to other users.
6. A user can be prevented from using them.
7. World Bank, World Development Report, 1994, p. 26.
8. See Mohan Committee (1996), Vol. 3, pp. 54-55 and 100-141.

10

Freeing Agriculture for Reducing Poverty

Sustained poverty reduction depends on rapid growth in both quality and quantity of labour demand. In turn the rapid growth in labour depends on rising output growth in agriculture and manufacturing. There is a strong association between output growth and rising real wages in agriculture and manufacturing.[1] Economic growth has also promoted labour shifts from low productivity self and informal employment in agriculture and services.[2] However, as discussed in earlier chapters, broad-based human development, especially to hither to neglected sections is needed to maximise the impact of rapid growth in output and labour demand on poverty reduction as well as to sustain growth. South East Asian countries have demonstrated the effects of such relationships where poverty fell sharply and labour income rose rapidly as education became more widespread.[3]

Poverty reduction largely depends on the labour intensity of growth.[4] Little additional demand is generated for labour from the capital intensity of growth and the situation becomes worse when inefficient industries are protected and investment is highly subsidised. Moreover, such development strategy eventually slows investment and growth because of limitation of markets and lack of competitive pressure to upgrade technology. At the same time, consumers have no choice but to buy poor quality goods at high costs and products being imported at high cost. These were the factors, which compelled India to initiate reforms process in the early 1990s. However, in spite of a decade of reform tariff and non-tariff barriers still remain high, labour market flexibility in the organised sector remains low discouraging creation of formal employment while the unorganised sector yet to be brought under the preview of labour, legislation, and agriculture remains the least reformed sector of the economy. These factors affect labour demand adversely.

The poverty reduction is possible with additional creation of employment opportunities *inter alia* the resultant of growth and its labour intensity. Naturally, a more effective approach to reduce poverty and increase labour demand would come only from a deregulated framework which will encourage economy wide growth and makes best use of vast human capital. Such a framework demands growth in agriculture and rural sector where poverty is largely concentrated besides encouraging exports and imports where benefits of comparative advantage is maximum and increasing labour market flexibility for growth in labour demand which will reduce urban poverty.

Agriculture

> Agriculture is a way of life, a tradition, which, for centuries, has shaped the thought, the outlook, the culture and the economic life of the people. Agriculture, therefore, is and will continue to be central to all strategies for planned economic development of the country. Rapid growth of agriculture is essential not only to achieve self-reliance at national level but also for household food security and to bring about equity in distribution of income and wealth resulting in rapid reduction in poverty level.[5]

This opening paragraph of national policy statement on agriculture has summarised the importance of agriculture in the socio-economic fabric. No doubt, since Independence Indian agriculture has made rapid strides. It has contributed significantly in achieving self-sufficiency in food and in avoiding food shortages in the country. Annual food grains production has increased from 51 million tonnes from early fifties to 206 million tonnes at the turn of the century. However, the pattern of growth has brought in its wake, uneven development across the region and is characterised by low levels of productivity and degradation of natural resources, resulting in widening the gap between rich and poor. Capital inadequacy, lack of infrastructural support and demand constraints[6] have continued to affect the economic viability of the sector in playing an effective and efficient role in reducing poverty.

The strategy of planned development that was followed in India during first four decades neglected agriculture and emphasised the development of industry ignoring the truth that it has been the backbone of the economy. Despite having achieved self-sufficiency in food production, the well-being of people depending on agriculture continues to be a matter of grave concern for the planners and policy-makers. The establishment of an agrarian economy which insures food for its people, raw materials for industries and wide market for their products, and also provides exportable surplus has failed to play its effective role in reducing poverty because of its neglect. Poverty in Indian—both rural and urban—has now become an effect and a cause of this neglect.

Without utilising vast untapped growth potential of agriculture, strengthening rural infrastructure for its development, promoting value addition through rural industrialisation, and promoting agro-business, creating employment opportunities and raising the standard of living of the people, poverty reduction will be elusive.

No doubt, agricultural growth has been a major factor in reducing poverty. Over the 1990s, agricultural GDP trend growth of 3.3 per cent per annum was similar to that in the 1980s and foodgrains production trend growth was 2.6 per cent per annum. Both were in excess of population growth, which was estimated at 1.6 per cent per annum. Yet rural poverty declined much less in 1990s as compared to the 1980s.

Limited impact of agriculture on poverty was partly due to declining agriculture growth rate in the northern and eastern States and partly due to shift in pace and pattern of technological change. These changes are both related in the inefficiencies in and unsustainability of the current pattern of public spending in agriculture, and to the limited reform in agriculture.

In a broad sense, approach towards agriculture during 1990s, was to subsidise power, water and fertiliser inputs, implicitly or explicitly, primarily for keeping foodgrain prices lower, including the costs of massive PDS that has been used also by non-poor. The equity, efficiency and sustainability were not the influencing aspects of the approach. The large-scale subsidy affected income distribution and demand for labour adversely and excessive use of fertiliser, pesticides and water caused deterioration in the aquifers and soil. An environmentally unsustainable approach was to some extent responsible for rising costs and slowing growth and productivity in agriculture.[7] Moreover, mounting subsidy has its impact on public finance. It "crowded out" investment in roads and irrigation and expenditure on technical upgradation, limited maintenance costs of infrastructure, and resulted in low quality of infrastructural facilities to the sector. These problems were severe in poor States where rural poverty is largely concentrated.

Although private investment in agriculture has grown but it has primarily grown as a substitute for lower public investment and deteriorating quality of public services which are highly inefficient and inadequate. The fiscal crunch suggests that subsidies in no case be allowed to grow as it would limit the capital and technological growth in agriculture. In addition, agriculture has seen less reform than other sectors of the economy. While overall reforms related to the trade, finance, foreign exchange, investment in industry and infrastructure, agriculture is continued to be constrained by regulations that limit price movement and inter-State trade, public procurement and canalisation of trade.

Freeing Agriculture

Great strides has been made since Independence in transforming the lives and livelihood of the people. Yet, nearly one-third of people are below poverty line and for more than two-third, agriculture is the main source of income. Agricultural development in the recent past is characterised by an extraordinary diversity in its pattern of growth in investment and productivity. Consequently, a growing prosperity among some groups is contrasted with deepening poverty among less fortunate. Winning the race between a growing population and creating an enabling environment for them to lead a long, healthy and creative life by raising their income and living standards is a formidable challenge. So it is a task of alleviating poverty. In a country like

India, growth and development is mainly dependent on agricultural development. Agricultural development takes place only when increased productivity and output are reflected in raising incomes and standard of living of rural poor in particular and people in general.

Improving agricultural performance will be vital for India's future development and increasing its competitiveness in the global market. Only feeding the people should not be the goal. Since agriculture accounts for nearly a third of GDP, the human dimension of its performance is far more important. It still generates 70 per cent of employment and 80 per cent poor live in rural areas. Hence, removing the worse of poverty will depend primarily on raising rural income and increasing productivity of agriculture. Planners and policy-makers are fully aware with this reality. In their own word: "Not only consolidation but also acceleration of agriculture production gains are critical for meeting the increasing demands."[8]

The Paradox of Poverty

Eastern India[9] is an example of paradox of poverty in plenty. Progress in the region has been slowest. A great majority of poor live in this region and work on land. Historically, it was the most prosperous agricultural region in the country. Many factors are responsible for the decline of its pre-eminence. Important among them are exploitation of the peasantry under the zamindari system, talukdari and sub-infeudalism, rising pressure of population on land and fragmentation of land holdings, declining of rural handicrafts, inadequate provision of rural infrastructures and neglect of the existing ones, inadequate provision of bridges, culverts and siphons in railways, roads and canals which interfere with the natural flow of water resulting in floods, water logging, perts and diseases, complete neglect of water management programme and resultant difficulty in adoption of modern technology in agriculture.[10] Because of these reasons. "Green Revolution" failed to make any significant impact in the region, though it has transformed agriculture in Punjab, Haryana and Western U.P.

The poor performance of agriculture in the region is generally ascribed to its physical, institutional, socio-economic environments which together determine agricultural growth. The

Report of the committee on Agricultural Productivity in Eastern India states that:

(i) The soil, climate, and other physical characteristics are primarily responsible for bringing about existing pattern of farming,
(ii) The high fertility of soil together with its wet rice ecosystem has resulted in growth in the number of farm families to such a level that farms have become uneconomic and highly fragmented.
(iii) The pressure on population of land has become more acute resulting in overexploitation of soil,
(iv) Lack of capital and inefficient use of labour, and
(v) The persistence of semi-feudal institutions.

However, these constraints faced by the farmers vary from State to State and even within a State as between districts, blocks and villages. The low productivity is not so much because farmers lack dynamism and motivation but because of their helpless dependence upon the semi-monopolistic public and private organisation. In fact, the system is inflexible and provides little scope for manoeuvrability to the farm operators. The poor input delivery system, low level of research and technical support, inadequate price incentives and marketing facilities have made them reluctant to intensify agriculture and diversity cropping pattern.

Economic growth is invariably accompanied by decline in the share of agriculture in total output, income and employment. At advance stage of development and growth, the labour force in agriculture tends to decline absolutely with the development of agriculture, producers gradually get moved from consumers and subsistence farming gives way to marketed production enlarging the shape for specialised marketing, transport, processing and packaging. These activities produce much more value-added goods and generate employment than agriculture itself. The increased productivity, made possible by technological innovation, and accumulated public and private investment has been also responsible for diversification of agriculture.

The Green Revolution which has transformed the life of its

people in Punjab, Haryana and Western U.P. has failed in other parts of the country because of

(i) the technology did not fit into the climate and soil of the region.
(ii) local research institutions failed to adapt the international varieties to local conditions.
(iii) adequate canal irrigation and rainfall was not available.
(iv) transport and marketing network were inadequate and inefficient and
(v) prices and other incentives were inadequate.

No doubt, there are host of factors responsible for the backwardness of the region and poverty of the people, the main cause has been the non-availability of social and economic infrastructure. The development of infrastructural facilities has not been adequate to accelerate the pace of social development and economic growth. But the shackles of agricultural stagnation can be broken only by massive investment in infrastructure and assigning allocative role to incentives in raising productivity. The farm entrepreneurs of Punjab quickly adopted the new variety because the incentives to do so were favourable. Instead of searching ways of spreading the success of Green Revolution, studies have been conducted on its unfavourable societal effects. It is true that wage could be found to spread the "Green Revolution" but at the same time it is impossible to spread without incentives in other parts of the country as investment is highly unprofitable for agricultural modernisation and raising productivity.

The Impediments

The success of agricultural performance has been caused by farmer's initiatives, expansion of infrastructure, and introduction of highs technologies mainly in rice and wheat, and adequate and effective maintenance of existing infrastructural facilities. For a while, the interventions by the government also have helped in spreading the use of new technologies and succeeding to provide a minimum food security for the country as a whole. Feeding the growing population has been the prime force in influencing the formulation of agricultural policy in the past and with the change in economic environment in the recent past, situation is gradually changing. Since agriculture has reached the limits or extensive initiation, the future productivity increase can come either from yield increase or more significantly from higher added values through change in crop patterns, deepening of agricultural processing and more efficient marketing. These in turn, requires a shift in policy both in production and marketing.

In fact, there is nothing wrong with market induced shifts from foodgrain cultivation to the production of other crops so long as the market reflects economic costs and benefits. Diversification of agriculture can create large employment opportunities than provided by foodgrain cultivation. The budgetary costs of State interferences have reach high proportions. Many studies have observed that only a part of the welfare transfers have reached the poorest. If the country wishes to subsidies food consumption for reducing poverty, it must be financed by taking the better off rather than through implicit taxation of agriculture.

The agriculture too needs reform like industry to compete with the world market. Perceptions that more sophisticated research about costs and markets will provide optimum solutions through administrative allocation have proved to be misconceived. No amount of research or administrative ingenuity will be able to remove the inherent contradiction in the policy and approach. Nor the bureaucratic fine tuning will come to its rescue. The need of the hour is freeing of agriculture to make it strong, efficient and competitive.

Constitutionally agriculture is a subject of State list, but the broad direction have always been set by the Central government. Time has come for the Central government to take lead in reforming the agriculture in accordance with the new Agriculture Policy.

In the change economic environment for playing its effective role in reducing poverty, priority must be given reallocate public expenditures in the sector from subsidies to investment and to improve the structure of production incentives by removing domestic market impediments and greater integration with the global market. At the same time steps be taken towards rationalising price support and stocking policies and reorganisation of food subsidy system to benefit only the poor. Reforms also needed in generating and disseminating new technologies, especially for non-agricultural crops, diversified farming systems and poor harvest facilities. Reforming infrastructure system in the sector for effective and efficient services, should be accorded greater importance.

Expansion of rural infrastructure, effective and efficient outcomes and comprehensive reform of rural credit and market incentives will increase income, generate employment for reducing poverty. Without such reforms, the financial viability of the system will not be helpful in creating an enabling environment for growth in the sector and poverty alleviation will remain only a pious hope.

Efficient and Sustainable Growth: The Guiding Force

Themes of agricultural reforms in the days ahead must be efficient and sustainable development with an emphasis on measures to increase the participation of the poor and the private sector. Efficient and sustainable development in my view, may not be possible without rationalising agricultural subsidies and correcting price distortion. It has been estimated that the explicit and implicit subsidies reach less than 20 per cent of the farming community. The farmers of the rainfed area receive very little. Rapid growth in subsidies have become a major drain on Central and State budgetary resources, often resulting in non-availability of resources for efficient operation and maintenance of agricultural infrastructure and long-term investment.

Trends in subsidisation are neither financially nor physically sustainable. A phased elimination of fertiliser subsidy and efforts to improve cost recovery in irrigation and power must become focal point of agricultural policy. Attempts are being made to move in this directions but it needs better sequencing and fastness in its speed.

The Policy Initiative

Agriculture has become a relatively unrewarding profession largely because of unfavourable price regime and low value addition. This has caused large-scale migration from rural areas. With integration of agriculture with global trade the situation is likely to worsen further if timely corrective measures are not taken. In the age of global competition, the establishment of an agrarian economy for ensuring food and nutrition to people, raw materials for expanding industrial base and surpluses for exports and a fair and equitable reward system for the farming community for the services they provide to the society at large must become the mainstay of reforms in the agriculture sector.

The National Policy[11] on agriculture is a bold attempt in this direction and tends to actualise the vast untapped growth potential of agriculture, strengthen the rural infrastructure for faster agricultural development, promote value addition, promote agro-business, generate employment opportunities, secure a fair standard of living for the people depending on agriculture, discourage migration to urban areas and face the challenges arising out of economic liberalisation and globalisation. During the coming two decades it aims to attain:[12]

(i) a growth rate of 4 per cent per annum;
(ii) growth that is based on efficient use of resources and conserves out soil, water and bio-diversity;
(iii) growth with equity;
(iv) growth that is demand driven and creates to domestic markets and maximises benefits from exports of agricultural products in the face of challenges arising from economic liberalisation and globalisation, and
(v) growth that is sustainable technologically environmentally and economically.

Sustainable agriculture has been the prime concern of the policy initiative which seeks to promote technically sound, economically viable, environmentally non-degrading, and socially acceptable use of vast natural resources to promote development of agriculture. Policy promises to take measures for containing biotic pressures on land and controlling indiscriminate diversion of agricultural land for non-agricultural purposes. At the same time it also promises to utilise wastelands for agriculture and afforestation. What is more important is the emphasis given to intensive cultivation.

The major thrust has been given to development of rainfed and irrigated horticulture, floriculture, roots and tubers, plantation crops, aromatic and medicinal plants, bee keeping and sericulture, for augmenting food supply, exports and generating employment. Animal husbandry and fisheries too have been accorded importance which will generate income and employment. Such activities will certainly help reduce poverty by generating income and employment.

This will be achieved by evolving new location-specific and economically viable improved varieties of agricultural and non-agricultural crops, livestock species and aqua-culture. For inputs management new strategy has been envisaged. Development, production and distribution of improved varieties of seeds and planting materials and strengthening and expansion of seed and plant certification system with private sector participation will be given a high priority in the future.

Consequent upon dismantling quantitative restrictions on imports as per WTO Agreements on Agriculture, commodity-wise strategies and arrangements for protecting the grower from adverse impact of underprice fluctuations in international market and for promoting exports will be formulated. Apart from price competition, other aspects of marketing such as quality, choice, health and bio-safety will be promoted. In order to protect the interest of farmers in the context of removal of Quantitative Restrictions, continuous monitoring of international prices will be undertaken and appropriate tariff protection will be provided. Import duties on agricultural inputs will be rationalised and domestic agricultural market will be liberalised like industrial market. So also, the structure of taxes on foodgrains and other commercial crops will be rationalised.

Investments in rural infrastructure has been accorded a very high priority as it has been starved of capital. There has been a decline in the public sector investment in the agricultural sector. Policy envisages to step up public investment for narrowing down regional imbalances, accelerating development of supportive infrastructure for agriculture and rural development. A time-bound strategy for rationalisation and transparent pricing of inputs will be formulated to encourage judicious input use and to generate resources for agriculture. At the same time, environment will be created through a favourable price and trade regime to promote farmers own investment as also by industries producing inputs for agriculture and agro-based industries.

Rural electrification will be given high priority as a prime mover for agricultural development and attempt will be made for qualitative and quantitative improvements. Building the gap between irrigation potential created and utilised, completion of all on-going projects, restoration and modernisation of irrigation infrastructure will receive special attention for augmenting the availability and use of irrigational water. Emphasis will also be given to develop marketing infrastructure for agriculture.

Institutional structure of Indian agriculture has been characterised by predominance of small and marginal farmers. Policy envisages to pursue-institutional reforms to channelise that energies for achieving greater productivity and production. The approach to rural development has been directed towards consolidation of holding all over the country; redistribution of ceiling surplus lands and wastelands among the landless people, unemployed youth, tenancy reforms to recognise the right of tenants and sharecroppers; development of lease markets for increasing the size of the holdings by making legal provision; updating and improvement of land records and recognition of Women's right in land.

With such steps rural poor will be increasingly involved in the implementation of land reforms and it will help reduce poverty with the increase of employment opportunities for the poor.

Freeing agriculture has been the main thrust of the policy. No doubt, the basic support to agriculture has been provided by the cooperative sector built over the years. The policy envisages to provide active support for the promotion of cooperative form of enterprise and ensure greater autonomy and operational freedom to them to improve their functioning. The thrust will be on structural reforms for promoting greater efficiency and viability by freeing them from excessive bureaucratic control and political interference, creation of social and economic infrastructure, improvement in financial viability and organisational sustainability and people participation through management reforms.

Freeing agriculture will allow the agriculture to play its role effectively in reducing poverty through expansion in employment opportunities and rise in income.

NOTES AND REFERENCES

1. World Bank, World Development Report, 1995, Chapter 2, pp. 16-22.
2. *Ibid.*, Figure 2, 3, p. 19.
3. The recent crisis in South East Asia, although painful, was small relative to the long history of benefit from growth, and left the vast stock of infrastructure and education in place.
4. A sustained increase in labour demand per unit of GDP.
5. Government of India, Ministry of Agriculture, National Agriculture Policy, July 2000, p. 1.
6. Such as controls on movement, storage and sale of agricultural products.
7. Chand, R. (1999), "The Emerging Crisis in Punjab Agriculture", *Economic and Political Weekly*, Vol. 34, pp. A.2, A.9.
8. Government of India, Eighth Five-Year Plan—1992-97, Vol. II, p. 1.
9. It comprises of West Bengal, Orissa, Bihar and Eastern U.P.
10. For details, see *Agricultural Productivity in Eastern India*, Vol. 1, Chapter 2, Reserve Bank of India, 1984.
11. Department of Agriculture and Cooperation Ministry of Agriculture, Government of India, July, 2000.
12. National Agriculture Policy, *ibid.*, p. 2.

11

Growth, Poverty and Reforms

India's trend growth of 5.8 per cent during last two decades of 20th century was the highest outside South-East and East Asia among large developing countries. However, despite such relatively high growth, poverty incidence was very high and its economic structure remained relatively unchanged. In spite of economic crises South-East Asia, Korea, Thailand and Indonesia has substantially higher per capita incomes and social indicators and considerable lower poverty than India, although the countries had similar per capita income in the 1960s. The experiences of South-East Asia suggests that India needs sustained, higher, more labour using, outward oriented growth, coupled with improved social delivery in order to reduce poverty.

Moreover, the sustainability and vulnerability of India's current approach to growth and development are a matter of concern. Substantial reforms in the early 1990s led to high growth. More recently, however, growth has declined while reforms had slowed and in some cases reversed. The key agriculture sector remains highly regulated (see Chapter 10). Export growth, which could provide more employment, has slowed not only because of slowing world economy but also because policies are reducing the profitability of producing exportable goods compared to imported substitutes and because of the deteriorating infrastructure.

These issues raises questions about nation's ability to the advantage of the next upswing in world growth, the domestic opening up under agreements with WTO, and the end of the Multifibre Agreement. The agriculture and urban growth face environmental problems. There is no improvement in the fiscal deficit which limits private investment through crowding out resources and keeping real interest rates high. Within the government budgets, consumption spending being increasingly financed by borrowing is further crowding out critically needed social and infrastructure spending. Large implicit and explicit subsidies and inefficient public enterprises deter private sector led growth and development and largely contribute to inequalities and inefficiencies and raise questions about the sustainability of agriculture growth that is so critical for poverty alleviation.

A rapid reduction in poverty and increase in growth will depend on a second wave of reform which is being realised by all.[1] As discussed in previous chapters, reducing poverty will depend on a comprehensive framework with improved access to the poor to education and health services, improved infrastructure, and provide good governance, transparency, a sound legal and judicial system, a strong financial system and human and environmental sustainability. Sustainability in development critically depends upon continued sound macroeconomic policy. The ingredients of sound macroeconomic policy are greater, openness to trade, encouraging more efficient resource-use and increasing labour demand to help reduce poverty. At the same time sound public finance and availability of efficient and effective economic and social infrastructure would enhance the capability of State and the efficiency of market for sustainability in growth and development.

The Growth Performance

The pattern and other recent developments, suggest that India's growth and poverty reduction continue to depend heavily on good monsoons and harvests. This dependence, coupled with inefficiencies and unsustainability in rural public spending limited the reforms in agriculture reducing the sustainability of its growth and development.

As evidenced from Table 11.1 in recent years GDP grew 6 per cent, one of the highest growth rate in the world and agriculture accounted for all the rise in GDP growth.

The GDP growth trend has always been influenced by fluctuating fortunes of agriculture. The trend growth rate of 5.7 per cent of 1980s was the highest outside South and East Asia

TABLE 11.1: GDP Growth 1981-99

	1981-90 Avg.	1990-91	1991-92	1992-93	1993-94	1994-95	1995-96	1996-97	1997-98[a]	1998-99[b]
GDPfc	5.7	5.4	0.8	5.3	6.2	7.8	7.6	7.8	5.0	6.0
Agriculture and allied	3.6	3.8	–2.3	6.0	3.7	5.4	0.2	9.4	–1.0	7.6
Industry	7.1	7.6	–0.7	4.0	6.1	9.3	12.2	6.0	5.9	4.1
Mining and quarrying	8.5	10.7	3.7	1.1	1.7	9.2	7.4	1.2	2.7	–2.0
Manufacturing	7.6	6.0	–3.6	4.1	8.5	10.6	15.0	7.7	6.8	5.2
Electricity, gas and water	8.8	6.5	9.6	8.4	6.3	9.3	6.7	5.7	6.6	6.3
Construction	4.9	11.6	2.2	3.4	0.9	5.3	8.2	2.9	4.1	2.1
Services	6.7	5.2	4.1	5.4	8.0	8.5	9.8	8.0	8.2	6.2

[a]Quick estimates.
[b]Revised estimates.

Notes: 1. Based on the new series with 1993-94 as base year.
2. Figures for 1981 to 1992 are staff estimates.

Source: Central Statistical Organisation, National Accounts Statistics 1998, and Quick Estimates 1999.

among countries with over 20 million population. During 1990s, its earlier growth trend rebounded rapidly returning to the post-1980 trend growth rate in 1992-93 and 1993-94. Led by surging private sector investment and production, it achieved an unprecedented 7.7 per cent per annum average growth rate. Thereafter average growth fell back to post-1980s trend and is below the significant rise in growth that occurred during 1993-94 to 1994-97.

The years of rapid growth were associated with greater factor productivity in a macroeconomic sense and a higher investment rate, which was also encouraged by liberalisation. The increase in productivity was because of more efficient use of resources encouraged by greater openness to trade. Liberalisation increased incentives to export and import substantially, raising the share of both export and imports in output. In a relative sense, resources shifted out of industries completing with imports and shifted into exports where they were more productive in a macroeconomic sense. Estimates suggest that on an average the productivity of land, labour and capital in exports is over 47.6 per cent more than in secondary industry.[2] Increased competition raised the firm-level efficiency of resource use which was reflected in more efficient use of capital. Protection on capital goods was reduced and FDI rose dramatically and there was significant improvement in domestic investment. In the macroeconomic sense, increased productivity was reflected by rapid growth of exports and increased market share during the first half decade of reform.

The recent slow down in growth may be explained partly by extension of the benefit of the first stage of reform and in some sense reversal of reforms. From a longer run prospective, 5.8 per cent annual average growth is relatively a good performance, however, it must also be recognised that 20 years of growth at this rate has not changed much the profile of the people. It has failed to create on environment for people, to live a long, healthy and creative life.

The experiences elsewhere suggest that sustained, faster, labour using growth along with inclusive education and health services will contribute to reduce poverty. India, Indonesia, Korea and Thailand all had similar per capita GDP in the late 1960s. However, the Asian misacle economies grew faster than

India from the late 1960s to the mid-1990s. Their fast growth reduced poverty dramatically with little worsening of income distribution. Because their growth was associated with higher investment rates and higher and greater increases in the average education of the labour force they were able to face the economic crises of late 1990s.

The experiences of East Asia suggest that India needs higher, more labour intensive growth and improved social sector delivery for reducing poverty faster. Key elements in increasing growth and reducing poverty will be further reduction in its still high protection, in order to encourage greater labour demand and more efficient use of resources and greater productivity growth through greater international specialisation. Competition; liberalisation of internal market, particularly agriculture and labour markets; improved infrastructure to better the links between domestic and international markets and spreading the impacts of liberalisation throughout the country and widespread improvements of social services will also enhance growth and reduce poverty.

Moreover, even current growth rate may be difficult to sustain without significant changes. One concern is the possible slowdown in total factor productivity growth in agriculture, associated with possible environmental problems. A second concern is the apparent slowdown in growth in the poorer States. Continuance of these trends would slow the growth of overall factor productivity and the rise in incomes, as well as push up the relative price of agricultural products to the detriment of poor consumers.

Macroeconomic stability and vulnerability to external developments are also important issues for sustaining growth. Large fiscal deficit and the increasing use of borrowing to finance public sector consumption still remain matters of concern as they increase inequality and creates problems for the poor.

Reducing Fiscal Deficit

Combined deficit of Centre and States[3] worsened nearly 9.2 per cent of GDP in 1998-99 and it had previously been among the worlds largest. The Central government deficit of 9 per cent of GDP in 1998-99 was the same at that of the crisis year of 1990-91. The revenue deficit at 6.2 per cent of GDP was substantially higher than that of the crisis period. No doubt, the Central government in their recent budgets have targeted fiscal deficit reduction to 4 per cent of GDP but it has remain optimistic in the pervious two budgets.

The high deficits have several adverse effects. They crowd out private sector borrowing, keep interest rates higher than they otherwise would be, raise risks of macroeconomic instability and crowd out public development spending within government budgets because of the high interest cost of the large stock of government debt. As a matter of fact, high fiscal deficits represent a risk to the development process and its sustainability.

From a longer term perspective deficit reduction was largely confined to the first two years after the crisis and much of the reduction came from reduction in capital expenditure. The revenue deficit has increased, since 1990-91 from 3.2 per cent to 4.0 of GDP in 1998-99, meaning that the government is increasingly borrowing to finance consumption. The Central government responded to the 1991 economic crisis initially by cutting expenditures on non-food, non-fertiliser subsidies and loans to the States and public enterprises. The high deficit in 1993-94 was mainly corrected by further cuts in capital spending and grants to States. In addition, wage costs were allowed to increase. Wage ccsts since then have substantially increased because of implementation of Fifth Pay Commission recommendation. During 1990s revenue expenditures remained unchanged around 12 per cent of GDP, capital expenditures declined from 1.7 per cent to 0.9 per cent of GDP. Over the last three years the Oil Pool Account has been a major factor in tighting public sector fiscal accounts.[4]

Domestic Oil prices were liberalised in September 1997 by moving them closer to international prices and providing for future adjustment. Consequently, the oil pool had a surplus in 1997-98 and 1998-99, a development that was helped by drop in international oil prices. However, since the middle of 1999, the oil pool once again began to run a deficit, as a result of the rise in international oil prices and delays in increasing domestic prices. In October 1999, government increased the diesel prices sharply in an attempt to correct the potential deficit in the oil pool. In the budget of 2000-2001 and 2001-02 many corrective measures have been taken but its implementation need political will. Post-Budget development and the experiences of the last year suggest that it may be hard to reach the deficit target. Trends in recent years suggest that revenues are less and expenditures are sharply higher in successive years. Some of the increase in expenditures is due to support and lending to the States in the form of advance tax revenue in return for fiscal reforms in the States. Also some unexpected defence expenditure due to Kargil war incurred.

Sustainable State Finances

Sustainable State finances will help reduce poverty. Unsustainability in State finances keep the Central government deficit high and reduce social and infrastructural spending which is critical in reducing poverty. The State's deficit in 1998-99 widened even more than that of the Centre and currently continues to be as high as the Centre's deficit. The magnitude of States deficit indicates that States can no longer be neglected from the standpoint of macro instability. Much of the State governments' recent and projected deterioration reflects the cascading down of the Central government's excessive 1997-98 wage increase. The widening of States deficit is largely due to the deterioration in revenue deficit. However, the wage increase has only intensified an underlying problem.

States fiscal crisis and their lack of adjustment, continuation of large inefficiency including subsidies, implicit and explicit, in power, water, transport and secondary and tertiary education. Users charges are low, collections are weak and costs are infected by overstaffing and inefficiency in the State public enterprises. In power, average revenue is only about 80 per cent of costs, reflecting low collections and inefficiency.[5] Regarding the other sectors, the States have also allowed irrigation charges to decline sharply in real terms. Charges for water are far less than the delivery cost. Similar is the case for secondary and tertiary education.

Subsidies encourage inefficiency and contribute to over exploitation of natural resources and misuse of budgetary funds. Subsidies are given in the name of social welfare. But its benefits hardly reach the poor.

Unutilised Tax Base

No doubt, States tax revenues have grown nearly as fast as income, their approach to the taxes induces inefficiency and limits the tax base, partly because of unwillingness to tax agriculture, and partly because of difficulties of setting up a value-added tax that would be harmonised with the Central government's MODVAT.

Perhaps most importantly, States' fiscal crisis severely weakens the fight against poverty, by limiting their social and infrastructural spending. States are responsible for over 90 per cent of economic and social infrastructure under the federal system. During a decade of reforms, they have slowed their spending

TABLE 11.2: Change in Social and Economic Infrastructure and Interest Spending 1991-92, 1997-98

States	Social[a]	Economic[b]	Interest payment
Andhra Pradesh	–1.4	0.0	0.6
Bihar	1.6[c]	–0.1	1.1
Gujarat	–1.0	–1.2	0.1
Haryana	–0.1	–0.5	0.2
Karnataka	0.5	–1.5	0.3
Kerala	0.7	0.3	0.5
Maharashtra	–3.6	–0.6	0.6
Madhya Pradesh	0.8	0.1	0.0
Orissa	0.2	–0.7	0.7
Punjab	–0.3	–0.9	2.3
Rajasthan	0.5	–1.8	1.0
Tamil Nadu	–0.6	0.6	0.5
Uttar Pradesh	0.5	–0.7	1.0
West Bengal	0.0	1.0	0.7
14 States Average	–0.1	–0.4	0.7

[a]Refers to total expenditure on health and education.

[b]Refers to sum of capital outlay and (gross loans to power, irrigation, and transport.

[c]The positive increase reflects a strong rise in current spending in education in the revised estimates of 1997-98.

Note: 1997-98 is revised estimate. Brackets indicate deterioration.

Source: RBI Bulletin various issues.

relative to GDP, as their subsidies have increased, transfers and loans from Centre have declined, and interest costs of rising deficits have ballooned.

Rising Deficits: The Matter of Concern

The large public sector deficit is a matter of grave concern in many ways. It puts the country into debt-trap. High real interest rates associated with large public borrowing generates a cumulative rise in the ratio of public debt to GDP placing the country into debt-trap.

Report on Currency and Finance is drawing the attention of the government that the present level of public sector debt is not consistent with the medium-term sustainability of fiscal policies.[6] Prior to the financial reforms that began in the early 1990s, increasing financial repression limited the interest costs of the growing public debt by directing increasing credit to public sector at low cost, crowding-out credit to the private sector and taxing financial intermediation. With financial liberalisation, the true interest cost of the high deficit become clearer. The interest costs of the Centre and States have risen by over 1 per cent of GDP since 1990-91. There was a fall in this ratio belying the debt trap worries. However, in recent years, the ratio of Central government debt to GDP appears to be rising. It rose from 58 per cent in 1996-97 to about 60 per cent of GDP in 1997-98 and 1998-99, which the Mastric Treaty Europe considers as a limit for macroeconomic stability. The ratio of total debt servicing to current revenues is estimated to have increased from 11.6 per cent in 1997-98 to 12.3 per cent in 1998-99.

Since the 1980s debt crisis, investors and rating agencies have a concern that government might resort to inflation or unsustainable foreign borrowing to finance high fiscal deficits and cut the burden of large domestic fixed interest debt, for one reason or another. No doubt, that India has one of the highest fiscal deficits in the world. In 1991 it suffered a run on its meagre international reserves in the context of a high deficit and despite its closed capital account. Brazil and Pakistan, having as high deficits as India, suffered attacks on their fixed exchange rate. However, because of its traditionally maintained macro stability, along with its large foreign exchange reserves and limits on capital mobility decreases risks of such attacks. Nonetheless, investors, concern will tend to increase the international risks premier and lower the bond ratings that India faces,[7] keeping interest costs up, even if macro stability is maintained.

India's large fiscal deficits and public debt stock also crowd out private sector investment, by raising interest rates above what they otherwise would be and reducing the amount of funds available for the private sector.

Much of the deficits could be reduced by reducing large implicit and explicit subsidies, which was estimated at 14.4 per cent of GDP in mid-1990s. Some progress has been made in recent budgets but much have yet to be done. In addition, the deficit could be lowered by further efforts at broadening the tax base, improving tax administration, civil service reforms and greater reliance on private sector which could be efficiently and effectively performed by them. India's sustained development and growth will be furthered by a reduction in the Central government deficit similar to 1992-93, combined with government realignment that relies more on the private sector and focuses on basic human development services, infrastructure and maintenance of competition and legal and regulatory framework to make that market work better. By not doing so, an opportunity has been lost which could have helped reducing poverty.

Much more analysis is needed on the 'how' of realigning government. In this context, a study of the possible paths to fiscal adjustment, taking into account the linkages between fiscal deficit, growth and poverty reduction and drawing lessons from international experiences would be useful.

NOTES AND REFERENCES

1. Sec. Conference Volume, Conference Indian Economic Association, Jammu, December 2000.
2. World Bank, 2000, *op. cit.*, p. 104.
3. Excluding disinvestments.
4. The Oil Pool Account represents the government's obligation to compensate oil companies for the difference between their

revenues from domestic sales and the costs of oil internationally.
5. Low collections reflect power theft, distribution losses, and increasing payments.
6. Reserve Bank of India, Report on currency and Finance 1998-99, p. V. 13.
7. Moody lowered India's rating from Baaz to baz in June 1998.

12

Development Prospects for the Poor

Following the economic reforms the last decade recorded a growth rate of 6.7 per cent annually. No doubt, this is an improvement over the previous decades, it is still inadequate to reduce the backlog of poverty. A veritable ICE* revolution together with globalisation of trade has increased awareness among the poor of how deprived and disadvantaged they have been and how the much improved growth rate in general has continued to elude them from accessing basic necessities of life.

The availability of education, health care, housing, water, electricity, cooking fuel, old age support, sanitation and employment are prerequisites for a civilised living. Such prerequisites are not available for a large number of people. For more affluent people, access to private schools, high tech hospitals, transport, communication, piped water and uninterrupted power supply may appear normal features of modern-day living. For the poor, the basic necessities of life have a different connotation. Their needs are limited to basic minimum necessities of life. They need minimum social infrastructure which include free and easily accessible school for children, midday meals at school, public health services, cheap public transport and basic sanitation and water supply facilities. Most of the rural habitations and urban slums do not have or have limited supply of such facilities. Inequalities, therefore need to be addressed through focused attention on installing and operating the basic social infrastructure that would meet the minimum needs of the poor.

Education, health, family welfare, nutrition, sanitation, water supply, roads and social security constitute the basic social

*Information, Communication and Entertainment.

needs. Government have been the main suppliers of these services everywhere. But providing these services have costs against which pecuniary returns are often intangible. These services are social goods which do not attract private investment. Naturally, government's expenditure is the key to creating the necessary environment and infrastructure that can render service to meet these basic human needs.

Social Sector Spending

As evidenced from Table 12.1, plan and non-plan expenditure of the Central government on various social sector services increased from a level of Rs.9608 crore in 1992-93 to Rs.36270 crore in 2000-01 (BE); an increase of about four times in eight years. As a ratio to total expenditure, the combined plan and non-plan expenditure of the Centre rose from 8.1 per cent in 1992-93 to 10.7 per cent in 2000-01. Expressed as ratio to GDP at current market prices, the expenditure on social services of Central government increased from 1.28 per cent in 1992-93 to 1.66 per cent in 2000-01 (BE). In spite of the severe budgetary pressures, the Central government has attempted to enhance outlays for social sectors.

Employment Generation

By and large, poverty and unemployment are the two sides of the same coin. Invariably poor are unemployment. Employment generation to meet the backlog of unemployed and the new addition to the labour force, is a challenging task. The increasing diversification of the economy accompanies by acceleration in economic growth has caused structural changes in labour market. Higher economic growth in the recent past have resulted in lower employment intensity. However, it is believed that this could be compensated by new and expanded opportunities in the service sector.

However as evidenced from Table 12.2 the annual growth in employment has declined from 1.44 per cent in 1991 to 0.04 per cent in 1999. The growth in employment has come largely from private sector. There has been hardly any growth in the public sector in majority of years since 1991.

TABLE 12.1: Central Government Expenditure (Plan and Non-Plan) on Social Services

(Rs. crore)

Item	1992-93	1996-97	1997-98	1998-99	1999-2000	2000-01
1. Social Services	6397	13659	15894	19729	23727	25873
(a) Education, Sports and Youth Affairs	1878	3988	5012	6550	7115	8416
(b) Health and Family Welfare	1722	2751	3174	3915	5110	5860
(c) Water Supply, Sanitation, Housing and Urban Development	788	2957	3304	4190	4619	5087
(d) Information and Broadcasting	371	593	898	1074	1230	1368
(e) Welfare of SC/ST and Other Backward Classes	488	833	725	946	1083	1267
(f) Labour, Employment and Labour Welfare	347	587	562	758	868	941
(g) Social Welfare and Nutrition	803	1950	2219	2292	3702	2935
2. Rural Development	3211	5081	5583	5403	5185	5397
3. Basic Minimum Services (BMS)* including Slum development	2466	2873	3684	4048	–	
4. Pradhan Mantri Gramodya Yojana (PMGY)	–	–	–	–	–	5000
5. Social Services, Rural Development BMS and PMGY (1+2+3+4)	9608	21206	24350	28816	32960	36270
6. Total Central Government Expenditure as per cent of GDP at current market prices**	15.8	13.9	14.23	14.6	15.5	15.5

(*Contd.*)

Item	1992-93	1996-97	1997-98	1998-99	1999-2000	2000-01
7. Social Services, Rural Development BMS and PMGY as a percentage of Total Expenditure*	8.12	11.14	11.26	11.24	10.85	10.72
8. Social Services, Rural Development BMS and PMGY as a percentage of GDP at market prices***	1.28	1.55	1.59	1.60	1.68	1.66

*Came into operation from 1996-97.

**The total Central Govt. expenditure excludes the transfer of state's/UT's share of small saving collections.

***Ratios to GDP are at current market prices (Base: 1993-94) released by CsO. GDP for 2000-01 are based on CsO's Advance Estimates.

@: Launched in 2000-01 (BE) as a new initiative for basic rural needs.

Note: Figures for the years 1992-93 to 1998-99 are actuals.

Source: Budget Papers.

TABLE 12.2: Growth rates of Employment in organised sector (per cent)

Years	Public Sector	Private Sector	Total
1991	1.52	1.24	1.44
1992	0.80	2.21	1.21
1993	0.60	0.06	0.44
1994	0.62	0.01	0.73
1995	0.11	1.63	0.55
1996	–0.19	5.62	1.51
1997	0.67	2.04	1.09
1998	–0.09	1.72	0.46
1999	0.00	0.11	0.04

Source: Economic Survey 2000-2001.

There has been gender bias in organised labour market. Women are known to work in the unorganised sector for low wages and at low levels or skills. Though in absolute terms, the number of women workers during the last four decades has more than doubled from 40 million in 1951 to 90 million in 1991. The percentage of women workers to total workforce have declined marginally.

Except during 1994-95 and 1998-99, the all-India average real wages for the unskilled agricultural workers have risen continuously and at an average annual rate of 3 per cent. However, as shown in Table 12.3, there are wide fluctuations among the various States over the years.

Poverty

Alleviation of poverty remains a major challenge before the nation. As seen in Table 12.4, there has been a steady decline in poverty over the last two decades, the total number of poor people has remained constant because of growth in population. Acceleration of economic growth which is employment intensive facilitate the reduction of poverty in the long-run. However, this strategy needs to be complemented with a focus on provision of social infrastructure for improving the quality of life of the people and economic infrastructure for gainful employment in

TABLE 12.3: Growth rates of Employment in organised sector (per cent)

Years	Public Sector	Private Sector	Total
1991	1.52	1.24	1.44
1992	0.80	2.21	1.21
1993	0.60	0.06	0.44
1994	0.62	0.01	0.73
1995	0.11	1.63	0.55
1996	–0.19	5.62	1.51
1997	0.67	2.04	1.09
1998	–0.09	1.72	0.46
1999	0.00	0.11	0.04

Source: Economic Servey 2000-2001, p. 192.

TABLE 12.4: Estimates of Poverty (per cent)

Year	All India	Rural	Urban
1973-74	54.9	56.4	49.0
1977-78	51.3	53.1	45.2
1983	44.5	45.7	40.8
1987-98	38.9	39.1	38.2
1993-94	36.0	37.3	32.4
1999-2000			
30 day recall	26.10	27.09	23.62
7 day recall	23.33	24.02	21.59

Source: Economic Servey 2000-2001, p. 194.

the form of targeted anti-poverty programme. Specially redesigned integrated anti-poverty programmes for generation of both self-employment and wage employment will help reduce poverty.

Social Infrastructure

Provision of economic infrastructure alone will not make any dent on poverty reduction in the absence of social infrastructure which includes education and health. No doubt, the National Policy on Education (1986) provides a broad, policy framework for total eradication of illiteracy and a commitment to make primary education free and compulsory up to Vth standard besides ensuring higher government and non-government expenditure, raising the percentage of expenditure on education to 6 per cent of GDP. Several schemes were launched by the Central government during the last decade to meet the needs of not only the educationally disadvantaged but also for the overall strengthening of social infrastructure for education.

However, based on the data available up to 1998-99, the Gross Enrolment Ratio (GER) for primary school children was 92.14 per cent in 1998-99 whereas GER for upper primary stage was still low at 58 per cent. The proportion of girls enrolment both at primary and upper primary levels continued to be lower than the gross enrolment of boys. Among the States, Assam, Gujarat, Karnataka, M.P., Maharashtra, Rajasthan and Tamil Nadu and high gross enrolment ratio for the primary level. It was substantially low in U.P. and Bihar. At the upper primary level Kerala exhibit the highest enrolment, followed by Tamil Nadu had Maharashtra. Again Bihar, U.P., Orissa, and Andhra Pradesh exhibit low GER for upper Primary level.

It has now been fully realised that women be empowered economically and socially to become a strong and vigorous force in the development of the country. Women and children constitute 67.7 per cent of country's total population. Empowerment of women will be beneficial for children also. To empower the women efforts are being made in terms of policy formulation and plan allocation for numerous project launched for economically empowering women.

However, despite vigorous attempts being made in this direction, in absolute terms the problems remain the same. No doubt, socially disadvantaged groups such as Scheduled Castes (SCs), Scheduled Tribes (STs) and Other Backward Classes (OBCs) have received special focus over the years it has helped only those who are on the upper strata.

Reforms with Human Face

When reform programmes were launched a decade ago, it was

promised with human face. However, at the end of a decade, it is no so. Recovery of users costs, as an essential ingredient of economic reforms have led in the deterioration of health of the poor. Privatisation of health services have resulted in reduction in access to health services for the poor and this in turn have adversely effected health indices of the population. There is a lesson to be learnt from this.

States exhibit marked differences in the social and economic indices, availability and access. Any cost recovery programme will perpetuate poverty if it ignores the hard facts of Indian economy.

Neither State is capable nor market is efficient to provide needed growth for removal of poverty. Since agriculture is the backbone of the economy, sustainability to growth and development will come not from the growth of manufacturing but from agriculture alone. Ours is a developing economy. It needs development first as it will create an environment for people to live a long healthy and creative life. Since planned development during four decades since 1950 had failed to create such an environment, we made a U-turn in our economic policy. The vision of achieving a higher growth rate in the new era was not aimed at benefiting only the rich or the middle class. On the contrary, the poor has always been at the centre of our development efforts. One must not forget the fact that eradication of poverty is not possible without growth. So also growth is also not possible in the absence of development.

How to make a balance between the development and growth for providing sustainability to the economy is a formidable task.

It has rightly been said: "nothing is more dangerous than an idea, when you have only one idea". The growth of an economy may take several paths, it is very tempting for political leadership to select solely in accordance with their own preferences, without regard to the preferences of those for whom they are or should be.

Rethinking Reforms: Back to the Middle Path

Nehru's choice of mixed economy as the framework in which development had to take place was not an instant decision. He took a long view of forces shaping India's destiny and in making his choice was actuated by certain basic considerations. Such as unsuitability of the acquisitive society to the present age and its replacement by a classless society, based on cooperative efforts, with opportunities for all, unsuitability of free market enterprise system for realising economic growth and social justice without the sacrifice of freedom and democratic right of the common man and existence of a direct relationship between economic activity and development of human character.

As a rule capital is shy and does not come in for economic development rapidly enough. This is true for both domestic and foreign capital. No doubt, it is not possible to cross the barrier of poverty, without an adequate participation of foreign capital and diversion of a considerable proportion of nation's current income to capital formation but the motto should be: "a fair chance a fair deal and a fair profit". This should apply to foreign and domestic capital. The participation of foreign capital is justified because, in addition to supplementing national savings, in many case scientific, technical and industrial knowledge and capital equipment can best be secured along with foreign capital. However, one should be fully alive to the political risks in accepting foreign capital. During planned era, we were alive to their risks. Speaking in the house of the people in 1952 Nehru observed that all foreign capital leads to economic dependence on other countries.

We must learnt lessons from our history. In view of our large cultural diversity and involvement of our people with religion and value system bequeathed by an ancient civilisation, the development strategy cannot avoid explicit dealings with values. We must involve sociologists in drawing up a visionary road map for the future.

If we assess correctly the gains and limitations of development during era of reforms, we will surely perceive that the basic structure problems of society cannot be passed and the sands of time run out sooner than we know.

India must not abandon the middle path—a path of tradition with modernities and follow the path of mixed economy to make State capable and market efficient for providing sustainability to growth and development for eradication of poverty.

Index